1 TIMOTHY

2 TIMOTHY

TITUS

Luke Timothy Johnson

KNOX PREACHING GUIDES
John H. Hayes, Editor

John Knox Press
ATLANTA

Library of Congress Cataloging-in-Publication Data

Johnson, Luke Timothy.
  1 Timothy, 2 Timothy, Titus.

  (Knox preaching guides)
  Bibliography: p.
  1. Bible. N.T. Pastoral Epistles—Criticism, interpretation, etc. I. Title. II. Title: One Timothy, two Timothy, Titus. III. Series.
BS2735.2.J64 1987   227'.8307   86-45403
ISBN 0-8042-3242-3 (pbk.)

© copyright John Knox Press 1987
10 9 8 7 6 5 4 3 2 1
Printed in the United States of America
John Knox Press
Atlanta, Georgia 30365

Contents

Introduction

Problems and Possibilities

There are three good reasons why the pastoral letters are so seldom preached.

The first is that they were written to individuals, not communities. This means that the almost automatic identification of the Pauline audience with the contemporary congregation is not available.

The second reason is that preachers do not know much about the pastorals. To some extent their ignorance is a direct corollary of the widespread scholarly opinion that the pastorals were written not by Paul but by later members of the Pauline school. For some a decision on Pauline authorship becomes a decision about the letters' value. Since Paul is the heart of the canon, the pastorals are not truly important. They can be understood completely in terms of the supposed historical circumstances which accounted for their production.

The third reason is that many contemporary preachers do not much like what they find in the pastorals. Seminary training in large measure confirms the contemporary ethos on certain points considered unassailable: egalitarianism is good, hierarchy is bad; women are equal to men and deserve an equal role in ministry; tolerance is the mark of maturity, and intolerance a sign of bigotry; wrongdoing derives from traumatized emotions not from bad ideas; the state, not individual communities or families, should care for needy people; tradition is stifling, but spontaneity is liberating. To a remarkable extent, the three letters of Paul to his delegates challenge these nuggets of conventional wisdom. As a consequence, what little preaching there is on the pastorals often becomes an apology for such an embarrassing gaffe by the inspiring Spirit.

Seen from another perspective, these reasons for not preaching the pastorals begin to look like three good reasons for preaching them. Take them in reverse order. Why do we preach from texts of Scripture in the first place? Is it because we want to find our presuppositions and preoccupations consistently confirmed? If so, preaching is a sham. But if we listen to Scripture because we believe that God's Word is different from ours, or that our conventional wisdom does not necessarily equal the divine wisdom, then precisely to the degree that these texts confront and contradict us, can we be quickened in mind and spirit. Do the pastorals say nay to our proclivities and platitudes? All the more should they be heard—and preached!

For the same reason, questions concerning the authorship or historical setting of the pastorals are not the primary issue in their value to the church. We read and preach these letters not because they were written by Paul any more than we read Mark because it was written by Peter's interpreter. We read and preach them because they are part of the canon of Scripture. This is a decision not of historical research, but of faith. And because we hear them read as Scripture, we listen not for what they can tell us about first- or second-century Christianity, but for what they say to our twentieth-century Christianity. Not the historical but the prophetic function of the text is the business of the preacher within the church. Does this mean as well that the work of historical exegesis is irrelevant? Not at all, for the texts of Scripture remain rooted in a linguistic particularity not our own but one of far away and long ago. The purpose of historical exegesis, however, is not the reconstruction of the past on the basis of the texts so that the texts' meaning might be "explained" but is rather the determination of the texts' possibilities for meaning so that we today might be "interpreted" by them.

As for the problem posed by the pastorals being written for individuals rather than communities, this too becomes a positive possibility for preaching. Because of the peculiar status of the implied readers of these letters—Paul's special delegates Timothy and Titus—the contemporary preacher is forced to struggle a bit more with the text, puzzling over the implications of this doubly mediated message. The automatic equation between Paul and the preacher, and between the Corinthians and the Californians is broken, and that is good. Now, the questions we ought to be asking all the time become unavoidable: is our situation analogous to the one implied by the text? Does what Paul says to the delegates apply to all of us, only to ministers, or to none of us? Which are the enduring issues for Christian existence in every age, and which are truly only of historical interest? In a word, the literary resistance of these letters provokes struggle out of which creative preaching can emerge.

Perspectives on the Pastorals

One of the most difficult tasks in preaching from Scripture is making ourselves ignorant again. Most of us are overburdened with ersatz knowledge. Seminary courses and commentaries provide us neat packages of information concerning each writing of the canon. Too often, the preacher knows already what the text "means"; the only remaining task is "applying it." Not surprisingly, much preaching on Scripture is therefore drearily predictable. Texts no longer surprise or shock us.

We make ourselves ignorant by allowing the texts to be strange. We let go of our packaged "explanations," and hear the words of the letters directly. Doing this, we are given new and exciting questions about the texts and about our lives. Is this really what the text is saying? And if so, what does it mean for the way we perceive our lives in the church? I take it to be my task in this commentary to assist my reader in reaching such a state of ignorance and alienation from the text, so that creative thought might result.

Here are some of the things I take for granted. I assume that my readers know the information about the pastoral letters they learned in seminary and can find purveyed in every other commentary. I assume therefore that my readers probably regard these letters as pseudonymous productions of a

Pauline school written years after Paul's death, to save Paul from the threat of rejection by Jewish Christians, and of over-popularity among ascetical heretics. I assume that my readers automatically look to the pastorals for tradition rather than charisma, polemic rather than persuasion, structure rather than spirit. I take it for granted that the slogans most operative in my readers' minds when approaching these letters are: "routinization of charisma," "patriarchalism," "early Catholicism," "sexism," "hierarchalism." I assume these perceptions in my readers mainly because other perceptions are rarely available in scholarly literature.

I am not going to debate such assumptions, even though I consider them to be wrong. I am only interested in allowing the texts of 1 Timothy, 2 Timothy, and Titus themselves to shake some of these assumptions. I invite the reader to allow his or her derivative knowledge *about* the text to be replaced by a direct and living knowledge *of* the text. The only way I can think to help my reader do this is simply to bypass the old debates and begin to treat these three letters as though they were worthy of the same sort of exegetical and herme-neutical engagement as the rest of Scripture. However daring, I want to invite my reader to take these letters seriously.

The one thing that can prevent this happening and, there-fore, the one thing I must spend some time on now is the odd assumption—held by virtually everyone—that the pastoral letters are really "one thing." Notice how our language gives us away: we speak of "the pastorals." But a handy means of cataloging often means as well assumptions about the con-tents or perspectives of three quite different letters. It is ob-viously prejudicial and trivializing to speak of the "outlook" of the pastorals, or the "church order" of the pastorals, as though all three letters were exactly alike.

I am not sure where this strange habit began (perhaps al-ready in the Muratorian Canon!), but I do know that conven-tional scholarly opinion concerning the origination and purpose of these letters has abetted it. In this construal, the three letters are in fact only a single pseudonymous literary production in which all epistolary features and personal ele-ments are but fictitious furnishings for the real purpose of rehabilitating Paul and advancing a domesticated version of his message. Wherever it started, the habit of treating all three letters as one fundamentally inhibits our ability to hear each text on its own terms. A few preliminary comments on this matter are therefore required before we turn to the text of each separate letter. In what ways are the three letters alike and in what ways are they different?

Similarities

The most obvious thing the three texts have in common is their literary form: they are all *letters*. This must be taken seriously for the simple reason that to a large extent form determines function. To read a text properly, we must understand the conventional and predictable demands of genre. We do not expect from a letter what we do from a gospel. We also know that each of the various parts of an ancient letter has its own literary functions: the thanksgiving at the beginning, for example, often anticipates themes developed later in the letter. The preacher should therefore pay close attention to the relationship of an isolated lectionary passage to other parts of the letter which are not read.

These are also three *personal* letters. Not only are they ostensibly addressed to the individuals Timothy and Titus, but their focus throughout is primarily on the personal attitudes and actions of Paul's delegates. He is concerned above all with what they are doing, and what they should teach others. On the other hand, the letters are not personal in the sense that they are simply the private correspondence of Paul to his friends. No, they are written from "Paul the Apostle" to his co-workers for the gospel. His concern for them does not dwell exclusively on their personal virtues but more on their ministerial character as teachers of the community, as "men of God" (1 Tim 6:11; 2 Tim 3:17), as God's "servants" (2 Tim 2:24). In this sense, no less than with Paul's other letters these are official in character.

All three letters, finally, correspond to an ancient epistolary type called *paraenetic*. The word "paraenesis" refers to moral exhortation, usually of a traditional kind. The point of such exhortation is not the development of new theories but the remembrance of traditional teaching. Not surprisingly, "memory" and "reminding" are essential elements of paraenesis, which encouraged the imitation of models for the learning of virtue. 2 Timothy is an almost perfect example of such a personal paraenetic letter. In 1 Timothy and Titus the paraenetic element still permeates the instructions given to Timothy and Titus for their respective communities.

Understanding the letters' literary form helps us grasp some of their emphases. We see why Paul wants Timothy to imitate him as a model (2 Tim 1:13; 3:10) and present himself in turn to his community as an example to be imitated (1 Tim 4:12); likewise also Titus is to be an example (Titus 2:7). The way polemic against opponents is used in all three letters also makes sense within this literary form. In ancient protreptic discourses that encouraged young men to become philosophers (i.e., moral teachers), polemic against false teachers was sometimes used as a foil for the positive delineation of the ideal teacher (philosopher). The polemic against opponents in these letters functions the same way. The point is the character of Timothy and Titus; the characterization of the opponents is the antithesis of the ideal they should pursue.

This literary self-presentation fits well the little we know otherwise about Titus and Timothy and their place in the Pauline mission. Paul was the moving force behind an elaborate missionary endeavor. Some forty persons—female and male—worked with Paul "in the field" as part of this missionary network. Titus and Timothy were important members of the team.

Timothy joined the Pauline mission early and became one of Paul's closest co-workers. He worked as an evangelist with Paul (2 Cor 1:19), cosponsored several of his letters (2 Cor 1:1; Phil 1:1; Col 1:1; 1 Thess 1:1; 2 Thess 1:1), and was his agent for several delicate negotiations (1 Thess 3:1–2; Phil 2:19; 1 Cor 4:17). Paul had great affection for Timothy, and presented him to the Philippians as a model for imitation:

> I hope in the Lord Jesus to send Timothy to you soon, so that I may be cheered by news of you. I have no one like him, who will be genuinely anxious for your welfare. . . . Timothy's worth you know, how as a son with a father he has served with me in the gospel (Phil 2:19–22).

We learn from Acts 16:1–3 that Timothy was of mixed parentage, with a Jewish mother and a Greek father. We suspect also that he may not have been personally prepossessing (or perhaps was still quite young), for Paul must tell the Corinthians "do not despise him" (1 Cor 16:10–11). Paul's description of what he wants Timothy to do at Corinth as his representative corresponds exactly with what we find in these letters:

> I urge you then, be imitators of me. Therefore I sent to you Timothy, my beloved and faithful child in the Lord, to remind you of my ways in Christ, as I teach them everywhere in every church (1 Cor 4:16–17).

Of Titus we know much less. He also had a Greek background. He accompanied Paul on a critical trip to Jerusalem (Gal 2:1, 3), and traveled to Corinth for Paul during the period when Paul was organizing his great collection for the Jerusalem church (2 Cor 2:13; 7:6, 15; 8:16; 12:18). Of him Paul says, "as for Titus, he is my partner and fellow worker in your service" (2 Cor 8:23).

The fact that both Timothy and Titus had a Hellenistic background, and that they functioned as Paul's representatives to local communities—to remind and teach them Paul's ways as well as be a model for the community's imitation—helps explain the distinctive language of these letters, which is so much more "Greek" sounding than some other letters. The reason? Timothy and Titus are being exhorted as *teachers*, and Paul uses the language appropriate to that task in the Hellenistic world.

Differences

For all their similarities, the three letters also have important differences, which should caution us against generalizations that are too sweeping concerning "the pastorals."

It is often asserted that "the pastorals" are concerned with tradition as a deposit. Actually, that concern is expressed only in two places, and its significance is not altogether clear (2 Tim 1:12–14; 1 Tim 6:20). In similar fashion "the pastorals" are said to be about church order. But 2 Timothy has nothing of that topic. For that matter, the arrangements discussed in 1 Timothy and Titus are also distinctive, corresponding to the historical situation each letter presupposes. In the case of 1 Timothy, a well-established community's affairs receive a series of *ad hoc* adjustments and comments; in the case of Titus, a new and unpromising group of churches is given elementary moral instructions for life in the household. The only thing said about "church order" in Titus is that elders should be appointed and that the bishop should be moral.

These letters deal with different opponents in different ways. The opponents in 2 Timothy appear to be members of the community who teach that the resurrection has already occurred (2:18) and infect others—especially women—with their doctrine (3:2–8). In 1 Timothy the opponents are people with pretensions to knowledge and learning, particularly of law (1 Tim 1:7; 6:20); again, they seem to be members of the community. In Titus the opponents are definitely from "the Jewish party" (Titus 1:10–11; 3:9) although their precise relationship to the community is not clear (1:13–16). Scholars usually lump these characteristics together. The effect is to rob each letter of its distinctiveness. Specific and difficult texts are replaced by an easy generalization.

In similar fashion, Paul's response to the opponents is slightly different in each of these letters. It is sometimes asserted that the Paul of the "real" letters answers his opponents theologically, whereas in the "pastorals" he only slanders them. The Paul of the "real letters", however, is certainly capable of slander against his opposition (see 2 Cor 10:12; 11:13–15; Gal 6:12–13; Phil 3:2, 18). Furthermore, one must look a bit more closely at the function of the polemic in the three letters; as I have indicated, it serves to provide an antithesis to the ideal teacher. Nor is it true to say that the letters entirely lack theological rebuttal. In 1 Timothy, Paul four times clarifies proper teaching in response to the distortions of the opponents (1 Tim 1:8–11; 4:3–5; 4:6–8; 6:5–10), a technique notably lacking in 2 Timothy and only suggested in Titus 1:15.

Paul's attitude toward the opponents and his advice concerning them is also slightly different in each letter. In 2 Timothy, Paul emphasizes an attitude of gentleness and forebearance. He holds out the possibility of the opponents' conversion (2 Tim 2:23–26). In 1 Timothy, there is no such hope expressed, and the treatment of the opponents is more peremptory (1 Tim 1:20; 4:2; 6:3, 20). In Titus, finally, the opponents are given very little room (3:10), and are to be "silenced" (1:11). Those who listen to them are to be "rebuked strongly" (1:13). Each attitude is consistent with the respective letters' portrayal of the community situation and of the opponents.

My remarks have had a simple purpose. In order to begin preaching creatively on the basis of these letters, we need to be aware of how little we really "know them" as texts, particularly as separate and distinctive texts. We must learn to treat them individually and directly. Only when we learn to do this, can we at last begin to be questioned by them.

Here are some things the reader should be aware of before starting to look at the three letters. It will be immediately obvious that I am treating them out of their canonical order. I have two reasons for this. The first is to help stress the individuality and distinctiveness of each document, to make each one appear "strange" again. If putting them in a different order helps, good. The second reason is that 2 Timothy shows us the form of the personal paraenetic letter in a pure form. By attending to it first, we can then be free to engage the distinctive elements of 1 Timothy and Titus without having to go back over the same ground again.

For each letter, I will provide a short introduction. Then I will discuss individual units of the letter. Some of my observations will be literary; I will try to show how the text works *as* text. Other comments will be of an interpretive nature; I will try to begin the process of examining the "text" of our contemporary life in the light of the text before us. The reader may be surprised at the attention paid to the positions of the "opponents." My interest is not strictly historical. Careful attention to the problem responded to helps us grasp the point of the text. Also, some of the opponents' positions are wonderfully contemporary. In all of this, I assume that my reader is a preacher, so I will not talk about the preacher doing such and such with the text. Most preachers surely know much more than I how to do that. Rather, I invite the preacher to enter into my process of reflection on and questioning of the text. Since we are reading letters and not narratives, we will not be searching out sermonic themes or topics, but will be asking questions such as "is he saying this to us?" or "what might this mean in today's circumstances?" Good preaching like good theology does not derive simply from information but from the struggle to bring the text of Scripture and the text of our shared lives into direct and sometimes frightening dialogue.

2 TIMOTHY

Advice to
a Beleaguered Colleague

Introduction

2 Timothy is the most personal of Paul's letters. Even more than in Philemon and Philippians—also written from prison—does Paul reveal something more of himself than his apostolic office. This is not the official correspondence of a founder to his church but the personal, indeed poignant, communication from a spiritual father to one he calls his "beloved child" (1:2). The text of the letter is interlaced with allusions to shared perceptions, values, and even desires. Paul holds Timothy close to him in memory (1:3) as one who knows his family history (1:5; 3:15). They share knowledge (1:15, 18), past experience (1:13; 2:2; 3:10), and present troubles (1:14–15). Much between them need not be spelled out but only suggested.

Paul's own situation is not encouraging. He is in prison, probably in Rome (1:16–17). He has already made one defense from which he emerged only like one "snatched from the jaws of a lion" (4:17). In contrast to his letters to Philemon and the Philippians in which he expressed genuine hope of release (Philem 22; Phil 1:12; 2:24), Paul here reveals no such expectations. He considers his life to be drawing to a close (4:6–7). He has no more hope for human vindication, only divine (4:18). Worse, he is experiencing from humanity both abandonment and rejection. Everybody in Asia abandoned him (1:15). Nobody stood by him at his first defense (4:16). Some of his fellow workers seem to have left him for other mission fields, while others, "in love with this world," have abandoned him altogether (4:10). Paul is therefore almost pitiably grateful for the ministrations of Onesiphorus who visited him in prison (1:16–17). He derives comfort from the expectation of a visit from Timothy (4:9, 21), his delivery of the books and parchments that Paul had forgotten in Troas (4:13), and the prospect of benefiting from the services of Mark, who will accompany Timothy (4:11). Emotional truth does not always correspond to physical truth. Paul is not in fact totally alone. He sends greetings to Timothy from some associates (4:21), and Luke remains as his companion (4:11). But Paul feels alone and abandoned, and that is what counts.

This perception of things is the more plausible since Paul's mission is also being threatened. The trials he had faced in the past (3:11) are not entirely over. Alexander the coppersmith did him much harm (4:14), yes, but also—and this is the important thing—he continues to "resist our words," so that Timothy, too, must be wary of him (4:15). Within the Pauline communities, furthermore, there is the social disruption and confusion being generated by troublemakers such as Hymenaeus and Philetus (2:17). Paul clearly regards them contemptuously as "charlatans" (*goetai*, 3:13) like those magicians who opposed Moses (3:8). Nevertheless, they are having a genuine impact, especially among the believers least able to resist them, uneducated women easily seduced by specious and flattering speech (3:6–7). Paul fears that the time is such that distorted teaching proves more effective and popular than the sound doctrine proclaimed by him and his followers (4:3–4). The opponents are indeed making progress (2:16–17). After a lifetime literally "spent" in preaching and teaching (4:6), does Paul face at the end not only personal rejection but also the utter failure of his mission?

Paul's mood cannot be lightened by contemplation of the character of those battling on his side for the truth. Our suspicion that Timothy may not be the strongest of personalities (1 Cor 16:10–11) is here given greater support. We learn that Timothy is in fact discouraged in the face of such opposition, perhaps even wavering in his fidelity to his work as Paul's representative (see esp. 1:5; 1:7; 2:1; 3:12). Caught in his own fatigue, fear, and fragility, Paul must somehow rally his beleaguered younger colleague to stand fast within truly threatening circumstances. That Paul could write at all is noble; that he wrote a letter such as this is inspired.

What sort of letter could—or should—Paul write in these circumstances? For some readers this is not a real question. Regarding the pastorals as pseudonymous literary productions, they assume the epistolary elements to be fictitious. It is common for scholars to term 2 Timothy an example of *testamentary* literature. They consider it one of the many "farewell discourses" written during the NT period. It is a type of literature developed out of the sort of bedside scene described in Gen 49:1–33, or for that matter, Plato's *Phaedo*. The dying hero shares wisdom with his descendants. In the Jewish version, this often consists in a prediction of the bad times to come, when opponents will flourish, together with instructions to stay steadfast in the traditions handed on to them by the elder. Some elements of 2 Timothy match this scenario rather well. But not so well as to be utterly convincing.

Quite another literary classification has more merit because it better fits the actual contours of the text. Paul had available to him a conventional epistolary form which admirably suited just the situation he faced. Later rhetorical handbooks reproducing letter samples call it a "paraenetic letter." A classic example is found in the Hellenistic moral writing called "to Demonicus." There, one who assumed the role of a father to a son reminded the younger man of traditional moral teaching, in order to rekindle his commitment to it. Such paraenesis was personal, for it was the individual person and not a community who was addressed. It generally contained three elements: memory, model, and maxims. *Memory* was important for the living recollection of shared understanding. What was remembered above all was the *model* or exemplar of the proper moral attitudes and behavior as found in a figure of the past or the present. The model in turn was fleshed out by means of moral *maxims* or instructions, which generally fell into an antithetical pattern: do this and avoid that. As we shall shortly see, 2 Timothy has these elements in classic proportion, so that it can best be termed a *personal paraenetic letter.*

Such letters were usually directed to the personal virtue of the recipient. In contrast Timothy is addressed not only as a "beloved child" but above all as a "servant of the Lord," as a teacher and preacher of the gospel (2:24; 4:5). Paul's reminders and the model he presents therefore have to do with the proper fulfillment of that role. This helps explain a feature of 2 Timothy which does not at first sight seem to fit within the category of personal paraenesis. Much of 2 Timothy obviously consists of polemic against false teachers. We will see however that the polemic is not aimed directly at the opponents but is used as a contrast to the positive ideal of the teacher toward which Timothy is to strive. Just such a use of slander was a feature of Hellenistic *protreptic* discourses which encouraged young men to follow the way of philosophy. In them, slander against opponents—which had as its first social context direct debate—found literary expression as the antithesis to the ideal philosopher. In 2 Timothy, therefore, Paul does not present simply a model of virtue for Timothy's emulation, together with a series of maxims saying, "do this but avoid this." He gives Timothy a model of the steadfast *teacher,* together with a series of maxims, saying "teach this way and not that way (in the fashion of the opponents)." The structure of the letter falls, therefore, into these three easily discernible sections: the presentation of Paul as model of teaching and suffering (1:3–2:13); instructions to Timothy contrasted to the manner of the false teachers (2:14–4:5); and Paul once more presented as a model of suffering (4:6–22).

How, then, should we listen to or preach this letter written long ago by an old man to his younger friend and colleague? In the most obvious way, the contemporary pastor can learn here something of the stern demands and ideal of Christian preaching and teaching. It is no mean thing to reflect again on this calling, nor is it unfortunate if the preacher preach first of all to himself or herself. But the letter need not have so narrow an applicability. By reading it carefully, the preacher discovers in this ancient witness many and marvelous insights into the meaning of the good news for all believers, for what Paul declared of his ministry applies as well to his letter, "the word of God cannot be fettered" (2:9).

Paul as Model Teacher (1:1—2:13)

The elements of the personal paraenetic letter are immediately evident in the first part of 2 Timothy. We notice first how Paul assumes the role of a father to his son. He calls Timothy "my beloved child" in the greeting (1:2) and in 2:1, "my child." By explicitly noting Timothy's female ancestors while neglecting the male, furthermore, Paul also places himself in the position of Timothy's natural father (who according to Acts 16:1 was a Greek). This is a comfortable role for Paul, since he regards those whom he has called into "the promise of the life which is in Christ Jesus" (1:1) to be like children whom he himself has begotten through the gospel (cf. also 1 Cor 4:15; 1 Thess 2:11; Philem 10). By assuming the role of a father, Paul also takes on the obligation of instructing Timothy in the moral life. It is his responsibility to shape the values and attitudes of his adopted son.

He follows the conventional approach to this task by employing the motif of memory. Paraenesis is not a matter of new teaching but of recollecting traditional shared values. Paul first "remembers" Timothy constantly in his prayers (1:3). As he does so, he also "remembers" his tears—the first hint to us that all is not well with his delegate. Paul also "remembers" the sincere faith held first by Timothy's grandmother Lois and his mother Eunice (1:4–5). Except for the repetition of the word "memory," this is not a strange opening for a Pauline letter; in other letters also the thanksgiving invokes the memory of those for whom he prays (see Phil 1:3; 1 Thess 1:3; Eph 1:16; Philem 4).

Paul's use of memory tells us something about its nature as well as about the nature of prayer. The memory he invokes is a form of *anamnesis:* not the mechanical recall of information from the past but the recollection of meaningful stories which shape individual and communal human identity. In this sort of memory the past is made alive and powerful for the present. It can therefore help to shape the future. Memory works the same way in prayer. By "remembering" the other before the Lord, we make them present with us before God.

Thus, Paul's "remembering" Timothy's tears means that he stands with him, sharing in his suffering, before God.

We would expect, then, that Paul would select from Timothy's past precisely the memory needed to shape his identity and commitment in the present. Timothy's tears suggest that he is fearful and sorrowful. Paul therefore recalls the "sincere faith" of his maternal forebears, adding "and now, I am sure, dwelling in you." This gives us a second glimpse of Timothy's trouble. Paul protests overmuch; he really is *not* sure that Timothy continues the steadfast loyalty characteristic of his ancestors. This is therefore the part of Timothy's past that Paul wants to make alive and powerful. "Hence I remind you" (1:6) is very strong in the Greek: "for this very reason." Paul's reminding is to "rekindle" the gift from God that Timothy had received. The image is stronger: Paul fans the dying embers of Timothy's commitment with fresh memory, so that his loyalty might again blaze into flame.

Verse 1:7, in fact, gives us our third indication of Timothy's problem: "God did not give us a spirit of timidity but a spirit of power and love and self-control." The word translated as "timidity" simply means "cowardice." The contrast is one between cowardice and power. Because Timothy is faltering in the face of opposition, Paul writes to bolster his courage and conviction. By reminding him of his past and of his present gift from God, he calls Timothy to his own best identity, so that he can act appropriately.

It is precisely this purpose which shapes Paul's own self-presentation as Timothy's model. Paul elsewhere presents himself as an example and asks his churches to imitate him in various ways (see 1 Cor 4:16; 11:1; Phil 3:17; 2 Thess 3:9). Here Timothy is to imitate Paul's manner of preaching even in the context of personal suffering. Three key expressions run through the section (1:8—2:13): "to be ashamed", "to suffer," and "the gospel."

When Paul says in Romans 1:16, that he is "not ashamed of the gospel" he is using litotes; he actually means that the good news is his source of boasting (see Rom 5:1–5; 1 Cor 1:31; 2 Cor 10:17). In the present context, however, genuine shame is the issue. If Timothy has grown cowardly in his work, it is because he is "ashamed" of the good news. Paul's suffering and his own make him waver in his loyalty to the task of preaching it. Paul's command to him therefore is, "Do not be ashamed then of testifying to our Lord, nor of me his prisoner, but share in suffering for the gospel in the power of God" (1:8). Two things strike us immediately in this command. First, it is not Timothy's own resources which will enable him to endure but the *power of God* which works through the gospel. We remember how Paul has already contrasted Timothy's personal cowardice to the power that comes from God's gift. The second thing we notice is that Paul's imprisonment is itself a source of Timothy's embarrassment. How convincing can this power of God be if the man who most emphatically proclaims it himself lies powerless in chains? Paul's imprisonment is an embarrassment to his delegate because it calls into question the efficacy of the message they proclaim. Paul's position is therefore awkward in the extreme. He must rally Timothy to new courage even as his own situation presents the most disheartening thing Timothy faces.

Paul must try to show how his manner of suffering demonstrates rather than disproves the power of the good news. Like Timothy (1:6), Paul was appointed as a "preacher and apostle and teacher" (1:11), and now he suffers for that very reason. But he does not grow ashamed. Why? Because he knows the one in whom he has believed (1:12), and is convinced of his power to preserve what he first entrusted to Paul. How can he be so convinced? Because God had demonstrated this power in the good news itself. This is the God who "abolished death and brought life and immortality to light through the gospel" (1:10). The God who calls Paul and Timothy is a living God. His "promise of the life" (1:1) is secure, even when circumstances would appear to contradict it. For Paul the ultimate proof of God's power is always the resurrection of Jesus (Phil 2:9–11; 3:21). He knows therefore that the fundamental pattern of the gospel—and by extension the pattern of Christian identity—is one that moves through suffering to glory. The power of God is revealed through the cross and the resurrection (see 1 Cor 1:24).

Timothy's cowardice was fed by his focusing on his own weakness and the imprisonment of Paul. He has forgotten the power at work in the gospel itself, the power of God's word effective in the world (see 1 Thess 1:5; 2:13). Paul therefore boldly presents himself as a model in 1:13: "Follow the pattern of the sound words which you have heard from me, in the faith and love which are in Christ Jesus; guard the truth that has been entrusted to you by the Holy Spirit who dwells within us." This extraordinarily dense statement requires explication by three observations. First, we see that it is not only Paul's personal manner of suffering that provides a model for Timothy to imitate, though that certainly is implied here (1:8–12; see also 3:10). Above all it is the "pattern of sound words," by which of course Paul means the gospel message itself. Timothy too must follow the path of suffering before glory, which the gospel itself presents as the pattern of God's power. Second, what is at stake is his very identity as a Christian and as a teacher. He is to "preserve what is entrusted to him." By inserting the word "truth" here, the RSV makes it seem as though the "truth" were some content of doctrine or tradition. In fact, it is the very same term used in the previous verse, where Paul meant the preservation of his ministry and personal fidelity. It undoubtedly means the same thing in this verse. The "truth" Timothy is to preserve through suffering is his integrity as a teacher. Third, he is not able to do this by himself but only by the power of God at work in the gospel, which Paul here explicitly identifies as "the Holy Spirit who dwells within us" (1:14). Paul's statement of confidence in 1:12 also emphasizes the "power" of God to preserve him to the end.

Not content with offering himself as an example, Paul now proceeds to present other models for his delegate's imitation. At first glance, the reference to Onesiphorus in 1:15–18 appears to be intrusive. Why should Paul make this autobiographical remark here? When we look more closely, however, we observe how carefully the recollection is structured. First, Paul places all of 1:15–2:7 within a framing which alerts his reader to its significance. In 1:15 he says, "you know," and in 2:7, "understand what I am saying." Paul wants Timothy to learn something from this series of observations. What is he to learn? Exactly what Paul has already been telling him: how he must "take his share of suffering" for the good news.

Next, the notice about Onesiphorus is structured so that it corresponds with Paul's previous statements. Onesiphorus stands in contrast to "all those in Asia" who abandoned Paul. Instead, he "refreshed" Paul by seeking him out in prison and serving him. By so doing he showed that he was "not ashamed of my chains" (1:16). As a result, Paul prays that Onesiphorus will receive mercy on that day (1:16, 18), just as Paul himself will be preserved by the Lord "until that Day" (1:12). As Onesiphorus showed mercy to Paul, so will God show mercy to him and his household (1:16, 18), for he is, in fact, a God of mercy (1:2). In a word, Onesiphorus has shared in Paul's suffering for the gospel and can expect a reward. Timothy should not miss the point.

In case he does, Paul continues in 2:1, "be strong in the grace that is in Christ Jesus," recalling again the empowering force of the gift (see 1:7, 8, 12, 14). With such empowerment, Timothy will be able to "Share in suffering as a good soldier of Christ Jesus" (2:3). He will not only endure but will extend the mission by teaching others what Paul taught him and enabling them to teach still others (2:2).

The image of the "soldier of Christ Jesus" in 2:3 leads Paul to a recitation of three examples for Timothy's imitation. They are stock examples from the repertoire of Hellenistic rhetoric: the soldier, athlete, and farmer. Paul also uses them in 1 Cor 9:6–24. There he stresses the support due those laboring in such occupations. The soldier deserves his pay (9:6), the farmer a share in the crop (9:10), and the winning athlete his prize (9:24). In the present situation, Paul emphasizes the other aspect of the examples: to gain a reward, each must endure suffering. The soldier devotes himself to the discipline of the service, not his own interests (2 Tim 2:4); the athlete must compete according to the rules (2:5); the farmer must work hard if he wants a share in the crop (2:6). When Paul tells Timothy to understand these things (2:7), this is what he intends: Timothy too must "take his share of suffering" before he can expect the reward of life promised by the gospel.

Paul has now presented Timothy with himself, Onesiphorus and three other examples of "not being ashamed of suffering." He concludes the list with the most important model of all: "Remember Jesus Christ, risen from the dead, descended

from David, as preached in my gospel" (2:8). Paul uses just
such a series of examples in another captivity letter. In Philippians he encourages a unity of spirit that consists in looking
to others' interests more than one's own. To show this, he
gives examples of such selflessness in Jesus (Phil 2:5–11), Timothy (2:19–23), Epaphroditus (2:25–30), and finally himself
(3:2–16). He then concludes, "Brethren, join in imitating me,
and mark those who live as you have an example in us" (Phil
3:17). Here in 2 Timothy the list concludes with the remembrance of Jesus "according to" Paul's gospel. What is Paul get-
ting at? Simply that Jesus also first suffered and then rose
from the dead and that this is to be the pattern for Timothy
as well (see also 3:12). What Paul wants Timothy to recognize
in the "faithful word" he now cites (2:11–12) is the necessity
of his participation in the very pattern of the Messiah: "If we
have died with him, we shall also live with him; if we endure,
we shall also reign with him." In contrast to the image of the
soldier, athlete, and farmer, Paul stresses here the element of
hope even more than that of suffering. All Timothy need do is
remain faithful and endure with Jesus. There is meaning to
his suffering.

Paul also recites the negative side: "If we deny him, he will
also deny us." This is a classic statement of eschatological ret-
ribution. In the present context of "shame," we cannot but be
reminded of the word of Jesus: "whoever is ashamed of me
and of my words in this adulterous and sinful generation, of
him will the Son of man also be ashamed, when he comes in
the glory of his Father with the holy angels" (Mark 8:38). If
Timothy "denies" the Lord he will in turn be "denied." But
Paul's own hope can never be confined within such narrow
mechanical limits. This is the apostle who declares that God
has shut up all humans in disobedience precisely so that he
might have mercy on all (Rom 11:32). For Paul it is unthink-
able that God's word should fail (Rom 9:6), "For the gifts and
the call of God are irrevocable" (Rom 11:29). So he concludes
in typical fashion, breaking thereby the symmetry of the
poem: "if we are faithless, he remains faithful—for he cannot
deny himself" (2:13). It is not Timothy's fidelity to God that
enables him to endure but God's fidelity to Timothy. God can-

not prove faithless to his own word and the "promise of the life which is in Christ Jesus" (1:1).

It is this conviction above all which Paul wants Timothy to renew in his heart. Just as Jesus suffered, so now Paul is "suffering and wearing fetters like a criminal," precisely for the sake of the gospel of Jesus Christ (2:9). But Paul is able to endure because he knows from the same gospel that a life spent for others has meaning, so that his suffering can mean gain for others. Paul's endurance is therefore not a feat of stoic athleticism but a process of being shaped according to the pattern of the Messiah: "Therefore I endure everything for the sake of the elect, that they also may obtain salvation in Christ Jesus with its eternal glory" (2:10). The point, we learn, is not that Paul is in chains but that the Word of God cannot be chained (2:9).

*   *   *   *   *

Having followed Paul's argument so far—and however personal and moral, it is an argument—we can pause and ask about the implications of what we have read for Christian existence in every age. Three topics in particular deserve some attention and provide the raw material for preaching: (a) the role of imitation in moral education, (b) faith as a human as well as a theological virtue, and (c) the coherence of call and gospel.

The Imitation of Models. When Paul presents Timothy with a series of examples both from the past and the present for his imitation (his ancestors, his teacher, his fellow worker, and the stock figures of farmer, athlete, and soldier), he unselfconsciously reveals convictions of his culture which are remarkably different from our own. Among those convictions were: that older people were wiser than younger people and had wisdom to share with them; that human life had certain repeatable patterns and was not invented fresh with each child or generation; that people learn values best from stories, especially real-life stories; that virtue and wisdom were best learned from the living texts of virtuous and wise persons. A moral maxim may tell us not to lie. But only when we observe the moral person in action do we learn the beauty, subtlety, and rigor of truth-speaking. The recitation of examples was therefore a staple of Hellenistic and early Christian moral education.

For a variety of reasons, it is avoided today. Perhaps this is due to popular perceptions concerning evolution and progress (the new teach the old, not vice-versa), youth, and individuality. Or perhaps it is simply due to a failure of nerve in the present generation of adults. It is perhaps not simply that we have learned to exalt spontaneity over structure—not realizing that the first depends on the second—youth over age, or the unique over the general. It is perhaps above all because to present ourselves as moral exemplars implies a realized virtue with which we may not be comfortable. At first, that sounds modest. More cynically, it might be suggested that to present myself as a model also demands of me a responsibility to *be* virtuous, with a consistency and comprehensiveness that I fear.

But the ancients were correct in this: people do learn their moral habits from the observation of role models rather than from propositions and maxims. So in the absence of powerful and positive living models of virtue, the young learn their morals from the examples of vice paraded convincingly through all the media.

Faith as a Human Virtue. In the beginning of this letter, Paul places particular stress on the faith of Timothy's grandmother and mother, as well as on his own service of God with a clear conscience like his fathers (1:3–5). He thereby reminds us of two aspects of faith that some Christian preaching neglects: that it is rooted in the shared human experience of trust and loyalty and that it is continuous with the faith in God found in Judaism.

Paul perceives his faith in God through Christ as continuous with the faith he had in God as a young child, that is, as a Jew. It is continuous as well with the faith his ancestors (also Jews) had in God. He makes explicit here what is found also in his treatment of the faith of Abraham (Gal 3; Rom 4). Christian faith is not first of all "faith in Christ" as a kind of confession, so that "Christian faith" is essentially distinguished from that of Jews. Faith is essentially a response of trust and obedience and loyalty to God, and it is the same response, whether found in Abraham, Jesus, or those who have received the Spirit of Jesus. For Paul it would surely be a distortion of faith and of Christianity to reduce either to its point of distinction from Judaism. He would not recognize a "Christianity" which defined itself exclusively in terms of a confessional "faith in Christ" rather 'than an "obediential faith in God."

In similar fashion, Paul asserts the continuity between this specifically "religious" faith and the faith Timothy learned from his Jewish mother and grandmother. Paul suggests thereby that the human context of acceptance, trust, and loyalty nurtures and educates the human person in the attitude and disposition we call faith. We see later that Timothy learned the Scriptures "from childhood" (3:15), as well. Faith, too, can be learned by influence and imitation. Indeed, we have learned to our dismay how nearly impossible it is for those who have never experienced a human context of trust to hear the word of God's acceptance of them in the gospel. Being born and raised in the atmosphere of rejection, betrayal, and neglect is not the best preparation for hearing the good news.

Surely there is no better justification for the understanding of the church as "the family of God" or as the "household of God" than this: precisely such a human community of trust and acceptance makes the message of God's goodness to humans credible. For the tendencies in Christianity which identify the authentic gospel only where it seems to reject natural human impulses or social structures, the oblique reminder of Paul in 2 Timothy is of particular pertinence. The gospel thrives best in the seedbed of human fidelity.

The Call and the Gospel. By no means, however, does Paul reduce Christian identity to a community of human loyalty. As emphatically as anywhere else in his letters we find here the insistence that Christians have been "called" beyond the frame of their merely human potential. He calls this a "holy calling." In the early Christian argot, this was shorthand for the origin and nature of Christian identity. It was based not

in their own achievements ("not in virtue of our own works")
but by "his own purpose and . . . grace" (1:9). In 2 Timothy, of
course, the particular focus of "the call" is the ministry to
which Timothy has been appointed. Both he and Paul have
been "appointed" (1:11), or "gifted," as preachers and teachers
of the gospel (1:6–7). Paul stresses first the "gift" aspect of
their vocation; their ministry was not a matter of natural selection on the basis of rhetorical talents or administrative
abilities or interests. Although mediated by human hands, it
is God's gift (1:6). The calling is in virtue of the "grace that is
in Christ Jesus" (2:1). For Paul to speak of the gift (or grace)
of God is naturally to speak of the Holy Spirit. So we find him
twice making this connection: Timothy was given the Spirit
(1:7) and the Holy Spirit dwelt in them (1:14). And as for all
early Christians, to speak of the Holy Spirit was to speak of
the power of God. Timothy has been gifted with power (1:7)
in which he can be strengthened (2:1).

My purpose here is not to recite a theological lexicon. It is
to show how far wide of the mark is the stereotype of the
pastorals as simply "domesticating" the gospel. We find here
in fact the hard edge of difference between human potential
and the power of God. The calling of Paul and Timothy is not
defined in terms of a human career or profession. It is defined
rather by "the life and immortality brought to light through
the gospel" (1:10), the "promise of the life in Christ Jesus"
(1:1), and the "salvation in Christ Jesus with its eternal glory"
(2:10). The hope by which they live and the hope they extend
to others is not therefore based on an adjustment within the
finite horizon of the world, a balancing of intra-psychic energies, or the proper ordering of society. It is a hope based in
God's own life, however inexplicable and elusive that might
appear to us now. It is for this reason that Paul himself can
have hope even in the most discouraging of human circumstances. His hope is not in his own or Timothy's human potential but in God. Therefore it thrives, in particular since
Paul had learned what Timothy had not and most of us never
do: that the path of those called by God must follow the one
who calls and that the gospel proclaimed also provides the
pattern of meaning: "if we have died with him, we shall also
live with him" (2:11).

Precisely these perspectives on Christian identity and ministry challenge in the sharpest possible fashion our too frequently habituated perceptions of Christian calling. To what extent do we in fact think of Christian existence in terms of the careful adjustment of intra-psychic and interpersonal relationships? To what degree do we in fact measure the success or failure of ministry in terms of its visible social or psychological plausibility?

The criterion may be the very issue Paul struggles with here: the experience of suffering. If the good news is proclaimed in a way that generates no suffering for the proclaimer or the hearers, we might ask whether it is really the good news which is being preached. If our understanding of life before God is one that does not encompass the depths of human suffering and sin, is our understanding in conformity to the gospel of the crucified Messiah? Paul found his failure and frustration meaningful within the pattern of his gospel. Do we?

Timothy the Teacher (2:14—4:5)

Having given Timothy several examples of patient endurance in suffering, Paul now proceeds to spell out by means of maxims the proper attitudes and aptitudes of the Christian teacher. This section of the letter is the most difficult for contemporary readers to appreciate, consisting as it does in extensive polemic. The path toward understanding must therefore lead through a discussion of the way polemic functioned in ancient rhetoric and the use made of it here by Paul.

There were many and competing teachers of wisdom in the Greco-Roman world. The great schools of philosophy (the Platonists, Epicureans, and Stoics) continued to propagate and defend their divergent interpretations of reality. Philosophy was not all a matter of scholarship, however, for the massive shift in social context accomplished by the empire made the love of wisdom much more a matter of therapy than of theory. Philosophy was regarded as a way of life, and the sage gave the most acute attention to the duties and virtues of the individual person. In the empire it was meaningless to discuss how the state should be ordered. Far more useful was the question of how a person should live.

Although some philosophers (like Seneca) were court advisors and others (like Musonius Rufus and Epictetus) were basically school teachers, others imitated the Cynic ideal of "freedom and free speech" with its street-corner haranguing of the multitudes. Some of these were undoubtedly drawn less by the love of virtue than by the "free, fresh-air life." Since the ideal could be camouflaged by pretenders, the issue naturally arose of who was and who was not a true philosopher.

Not surprisingly, philosophers challenged each other not so much on the adequacy of their theories as on how well they lived up to their professed ideals. The basic way to attack another school was to say that it preached but did not practice. Alternatively, its practice showed that its theory was wrong. Stoics would thus claim that the Epicurean denial of providence led logically to immorality; Platonists could contend that the Cynics' rejection of custom led to the collapse of the social order. To attack the morals of another philosopher, then, was to attack his ideas as well. The function of polemic was to discredit the teaching of an opponent. The literature of the Hellenistic age is filled with such polemic, revealing to us in the process the figure of the "charlatan" (*goes*), someone who has the form of the sage but not the reality. Like the would-be Cynics who grew beards, wandered with staff and rough cloak, and learned to vituperate others without any real virtue of their own, all charlatans were regarded as show without substance. Such philosophic flimflam men could charm the simple and gullible but were incapable of giving them anything of lasting value. The *goes* was therefore regarded as a dangerous if eccentric parody of the philosopher and was a frequent object of contempt (see Lucian's *Timon*).

So common was this sort of polemic that it quickly became stereotyped. No matter the specific allegiances of one's opponents, they were by definition charlatans who preached but did not practice. They all exemplified the classic threefold categories of vice: they were lovers of pleasure, lovers of money, lovers of glory. Their minds were corrupt. They were ignorant and their teachings destructive. Cynics in particular were perceived as a threat to the social order because they encouraged others to throw off the traces to enjoy the "free-dom and free speech," which their critics saw as license. Discovering the specific characteristics of opposing teachers is sometimes therefore difficult. Real life figures can only be glimpsed between the lines of the stereotype.

In Paul's other letters, he uses similar polemic against his rivals. He refers to those he calls "enemies of the cross" in this fashion: "Their end is destruction, their god is the belly, and they glory in their shame, with minds set on earthly things" (Phil 3:19). He charges the "judaizers" in Galatia with preaching without practicing: "even those who receive circumcision do not themselves keep the law" (Gal 6:13). His rivals for the affection and allegiance of the Corinthian community are "without understanding" (2 Cor 10:12). They are "false apostles, deceitful workmen, disguising themselves as apostles of Christ" (2 Cor 11:13). They are boastful (11:18). They "make slaves" of their hearers (11:20). They are in allegiance with Satan as they seduce Paul's community (11:3). We meet the motifs of "ignorance," of "making slaves," and of "the devil" again here in 2 Timothy.

A secondary use of polemic is also well-attested in Hellenistic literature. It is found in the protreptic discourses written to encourage young men to take up the way of philosophy. In such discourses the model of the ideal philosopher (such as Socrates or Diogenes) was presented for imitation. Then the ideals of the philosophic life were spelled out by means of contrast to the qualities of the charlatans. Frequently the negative and positive images were arranged antithetically, as in Lucian's *Demonax* or in Epictetus' *Discourse* III, 23.

It is the second use of polemic we meet in 2 Timothy 2:14—4:5. Paul addresses Timothy as a preacher and teacher, as well as one who is to instruct others how to teach (2:2). Timothy is therefore to "remind" them of the attitudes and actions which should be theirs as teachers (2:14), just as Paul has been "reminding" Timothy, and in fact does so here again under the guise of instructions for others. We notice that after his initial statement warning those Timothy is to instruct (2:14), Paul shifts immediately to the singular second person imperative: "present yourself to God" (2:15). In fact, it is Timothy who is the object of Paul's instructions throughout this section. There is a regular alternation of polemic describing the negative practices Timothy is to avoid (2:14, 16–17, 23; 3:2–9, 13; 4:3–4), with positive instructions to Timothy, "but you, do this" (2:15, 22, 24; 3:10, 14; 4:1–2, 5). The pattern is interrupted only by short digressions (2:19–21, 25–26; 3:15–16), and is concluded by the final solemn charge to Timothy: "you always be steady, endure suffering, do the work of an evangelist, fulfill your ministry" (4:5). The function of the polemic in 2 Timothy is therefore not directly to discredit the opponents (Timothy did not need that) but to present the dark shadow of the ideal Timothy himself is to pursue.

We do not conclude from this literary arrangement that the opponents were not real; they obviously were. But the literary function warns us to be careful in sorting out what is typical of all charlatans and what is unique to the rivals of Paul and Timothy.

What impression of the false teachers is given by Paul's polemic? We will move from the most general characterizations to the most specific. In the broadest sense, of course, they are simply "the opponents" (2:25). Paul places them in a category of derision by calling them "charlatans" (*goetai*, 3:13). We expect them to be preachers without practice and are not surprised when Paul tells us that they are "holding the form of religion but denying the power of it" (3:5). But because of their appearance they can fool the unwary; they are, therefore, "deceivers" (3:13).

Paul has little respect for their ideas or their intelligence. They have "swerved from the truth" (2:18); they are foolish (2:23), "of corrupt mind and counterfeit faith" (3:8). They are ignorant (3:9). They peddle myths (4:4). They not only deceive others; they are themselves deceived (3:13).

In the ancient world, it would follow from such corruption of mind that their morals also would be corrupt. Although they pretend to be religious, they are actually godless (2:16) and wicked (3:13), if not also subversive (2:22). The long list of vices in 3:2–4 includes the classic triad: they are lovers of self (vainglory), lovers of money, and lovers of pleasure. Such vice-lists are ordinarily stock and predictable. This one, however, is notable for its focus on misanthropic vices: they are "proud, arrogant, abusive . . . inhuman, implacable . . . fierce, haters of good, treacherous, reckless. . . ." This concentration suggests that Timothy's opponents belong to the category of sages who specialized in harshness. Their misanthropy paraded as a hatred of vice and luxury.

This suggestion is given support by their style of teaching. To the stereotype we can perhaps chalk up the charge that they pander to their hearers (4:3), are deceptive (3:13), and teach myths (4:4). All false teachers do that. Neither can we gain much specific information from the charge that their teaching is "empty and profane" (2:16). To call their teaching "useless," likewise, is to state the obvious, for in the realm of Hellenistic moral discourse, to be "useless" was the very essence of false teaching (see James 2:14–16). More helpful is the characterization of their teaching as a "disputing about words" (literally, "word chopping," 2:14), and "controversies [that] breed quarrels" (2:23). Their style matches the harshness of their vices. The opposing teachers are harsh and disputatious.

Because the opponents are not really philosophers but religious teachers, their allegiances are defined in terms taken from the symbolic world of Torah. They are working for Satan or at least have been caught in "the snare of the devil" (2:26). They stand in the tradition of the apocryphal Egyptian magicians Jannes and Jambres who opposed Moses at the court of Pharaoh (see Exod 7:11). The difference between Moses and those magicians was the source of their power: Moses' came from God, theirs from technique. Moses therefore liberated the people; the magicians were shamed. Just so, Paul says, the wizardry of these opponents will quickly be made plain to all as foolishness (3:9).

Still, there is obvious reason for concern. Even though Paul declares, "they will not get very far" (3:9), the opposition is already enjoying considerable success. Paul says candidly in 2:16 that they are advancing ever more in godlessness, and in 3:13 he remarks again on their progression "from bad to worse." In Hellenistic moral discourse, vice was often compared to disease, as virtue was to health. The true philosopher was therefore a "physician of souls" who could diagnose vice and provide guidance to virtue. Paul gives Timothy a vivid image both of the opponents' teaching and its success when he says "their talk [spreads] like gangrene" (2:17). If they were not enjoying success, in fact, there would be no need to take notice of them or so carefully craft advice to Timothy in contrast to them and their methods. As it is, Paul says that they are "upsetting the faith of some" (2:18). Paul obviously thinks this is by "deception" (3:13), but he recognizes that they are having a real impact on the stability of the community.

The precise target of the opposing teachers (including, we remember, Hymenaeus and Philetus, 2:17) were those Paul calls *gynaikaria* (3:6). It is not a particularly pleasant term, and English translations make it even more offensive to contemporary ears. It is important, therefore, to see exactly what Paul is and is not saying. If there is scandal, it should at least be properly identified.

Paul is clearly not a misogynist in this letter; we have seen already that he praises Lois and Eunice for the role they played in Timothy's upbringing (1:5; 3:15). Nor is he really properly sexist. He does not say that women are "silly" or "weak" (ways *gynaikaria* is often translated) as a class of people. In certain contexts, of course, the term can have those connotations. And even by itself, it at least bears the male condescension of our term "the little woman" (see, for example, Epictetus, *Encheiridion*, 7). It is clear, however, that Paul has specific sorts of women in mind, not all the women in the world. He says that they are "burdened with sins and swayed by various impulses, who will listen to anybody and can never arrive at a knowledge of the truth" (3:6–7). He is obviously not describing the nature of women but the problems of the women of a certain wealth and social position in the ancient world. The closest contemporary analogy would be those women of a certain age and class so gently parodied by Helen Hokinson in her New Yorker cartoons; women of means and mobility but without real education or real power in the world, and therefore, however much they take themselves and their many projects seriously, are regarded by observers as "silly."

Paul does not say that women as such "listen to anybody and cannot learn the truth." Instead, we here meet the wealthy leisured woman who has time for the pursuit of "wisdom" but whose education does not enable her to distinguish the genuine from the false. She is therefore the "perpetual student" of philosophy or theosophy. This sort of woman was ready prey for the charlatans who came into her house, willing to be charmed by their appearance and the rigor and harshness of their message, "being made slaves" by their teachings. In fact such women of position and means have often been so seduced, never more clearly so than in the case of the Czarina of Russia and the monk Rasputin. So clear is the historical record that Paul ought to be relieved from the burden of being a slanderer of women and praised for his acute diagnosis of the techniques of religious proselytism.

A few final remarks on this ticklish passage. Paul is not saying that being a woman makes one prey to falsehood. Rather it is being undereducated and deprived of useful employment which makes one vulnerable in this way. It would betray Paul's intention to deduce that women are in fact "incapable of learning." Paul has already stated how they taught Timothy the most important truths of faith and the Scripture. It would be equally unfaithful to the text to conclude that women as a class of people should be prevented from being educated, or from leadership roles in the church, for the passage suggests that to some degree their problem was precisely lack of education and responsibility. More on this particular issue, when we come to the even more difficult passage in 1 Timothy.

We arrive finally at the only specific thing mentioned about the opponents' teaching. They were saying that "the resurrection is past already" (2:18). But what does this mean, and why should it be a teaching particularly attractive to the "little women" in households? Paul would obviously wholeheartedly agree that the resurrection of Jesus had already occurred. The only point of reference would therefore have to be the "resurrection of the just" which in the apocalyptic scenario meant the beginning of the age to come. In what sense could this be asserted or denied?

Surely no one was claiming that the resurrection had occured as a cosmic, historical event, for in its Christian version that expectation involved the return of the Son of man. These teachers must therefore have understood the "resurrection" as a present state of spiritual transformation which enabled believers to participate already in the "angelic life" associated with the resurrection (see Luke 20:34–36). Just this sort of understanding was active in Paul's Corinthian congregation. Paul sharply rebuked some in that community and reminded them that the gift of the Spirit did not mean that they already partook in the life of the kingdom, much less "rule" in it (1 Cor 4:8). He told them that our present "flesh and blood" could not inherit eternal life, and that we all must be changed (1 Cor 15:50–51).

In Corinth, a "realized eschatology" led to attitudes of spiritual elitism and enthusiasm. It also led among some to the breakdown of moral standards, and the rejection of social conventions. It also appeared to lead to several forms of sexual expression. Among some it led to promiscuity. If the body had no future, it made sense to treat it indiscriminately (1 Cor 6:16). For others, the "angelic life" apparently demanded abstention from sex altogether, leading to the slogan "it is well . . . not to touch a woman" (1 Cor 7:1). Paul rejected altogether the option of sexual promiscuity. The option of celibacy he strongly qualified, allowing it for the sake of the mission, but also insisting that marriage was indissoluble except under the most extraordinary circumstances (1 Cor 7:10–11).

Could any of these options have had particular appeal to the leisured women of households who were chronically open to esoteric teachings? Paul's phrase "driven by various impulses" bears a sexual connotation, and it is easy to see something more than spiritual seduction taking place. But he also lists "burdened with sins." It would appear that a version of realized eschatology which made celibacy the norm for the Christian life would have a strong attraction for such women. It would offer them two things: freedom from the guilt and desires associated with sexual drives, and also perhaps, freedom from the obligations of the household.

One way of picturing the ideal Paul presents to Timothy is simply to reverse everything negative said about the opponents. Many of the commands directed at the delegate are negative: he is to "avoid," "shun," "not do" what the opponents do (2:14, 16, 22, 23, 24; 3:5). There is even a different spatial image for Timothy. While the opponents are said to "advance" and "make progress," Timothy is to "stand fast" and "be steady" (3:14; 4:5). In contrast to their life of vice, Timothy is to "pursue" virtues such as "[justice], faith, love, and peace" (2:22). Rather than be avid for "novel desires," Timothy is to align himself with "those who call upon the Lord from a pure heart" (2:22, 19), and "all who desire to live a godly life in Christ Jesus" (3:12). In a word, he is to affirm the shared traditions of the community he serves. We cannot picture Timothy sneaking into houses for purposes of seduction; his ministry is open and sincere and addressed to all.

Most of all Timothy is not to define himself or his message in terms of his hearers' expectations, as would a mere rhetorician or sophist. Those expectations themselves could be volatile and unworthy (4:3–4). He is rather to be a servant of God (2:24) and work as one answerable to God. He seeks therefore to be "approved" by God and an unashamed workman (2:15)—we notice the reminder of "shame," picked up from chapter one. In contrast to the charlatans who are themselves deceived even as they deceive, he "rightly handles the word of truth." For the expression, "rightly handle," Paul uses another medical term whose exact meaning is somewhat obscure, but which seems to involve the act of cutting or surgery—a stark image in contrast to the spread of gangrene! For Paul the battle here truly is one for "the truth" (2:15, 18, 25; 3:7–8; 4:4) even as it is elsewhere in his letters (see Gal 2:5, 14; 5:7; 2 Cor 13:8; Eph 4:21–25; Col 1:5–6; 2 Thess 2:12). The truth in question goes far beyond doctrinal niceties. It involves the integrity of the Christian experience and the authentic expression of the gift received from God. It is much more an existential than an abstract truth. It means living in accord with God's claim on the world.

Paul therefore emphasizes that Timothy is answerable to God as judge. In 2:21 he calls the vessel which is cleansed from sinners and holy, "useful to the master." And his final charge to Timothy is made before "God and ... Christ Jesus who is to judge the living and the dead, and by his appearing and his kingdom" (4:1). Because he is answerable to God—and is empowered by him—Timothy can "fulfil your ministry" and "do the work of an evangelist" (4:5); he can "preach

the word, be urgent, convince, rebuke, exhort" (4:2). Notice
that he has not just one way of preaching. He fits the speech
to the need: for this person, rebuke; for that one, persuasion.
Not their desires but their needs dictate a flexibility in style.
And because he is not dependent for his success on the response of the listeners, he can do this faithfully "in season and
out of season" (4:2); not circumstances but the truth of God's
word shapes his preaching and teaching. Timothy will not
therefore—at least ideally—be swayed by adverse circumstances or the success of the opposition.

The most striking contrast to the false teachers, however, is
found in the manner of Timothy's teaching. In his final
charge, Paul reminds him to be "unfailing in patience and in
teaching" (4:2). The phrase could equally be translated, "un-
failingly patient in your teaching." The word for patience here
is not the ordinary one meaning "endurance," but rather a
term which connotes "tolerance, long-suffering, magnanim-
ity." Even in the face of opposition and rejection, Timothy is
not to respond in kind, growing crabbed and spiteful. He is
not to imitate the bellicose words and hostile attitudes of the
opponents. Paul tells him explicitly that: "the Lord's servant
must not be quarrelsome but kindly to every one, an apt
teacher, forbearing, correcting his opponents with gentleness" (2:25). By advocating gentleness in teaching, Paul is
faithful to his own manner in his churches. Among the Thes-
salonians Paul says he was "gentle . . . like a nurse" (1 Thess
2:7)—again the use of medical imagery! With the refractory
Corinthians Paul claims that he was meek "with the meekness and gentleness of Christ" (2 Cor 10:1); so much so that
the Corinthians took advantage of it. Paul also here aligns
Timothy with those moral teachers who regarded vice as best
cured not by cautery or surgery but by the gentler arts of
persuasion and care. Paul is not interested in winning a war
of words. He wants to convert and heal even the harsh
opponents.

The possibility of change (or repentance) is suggested already by Paul's image of the great house containing both precious and lowly vessels (2:20–21). As in his other use of this
metaphor (Rom 9:20–23), things get a bit complex, but the
central point is clear enough. Pots don't change, people can:

"If any one purifies himself from what is ignoble, then he will be a vessel for noble use, consecrated and useful [notice the term "useful" again] to the master of the house, ready for any good work" (2:21). Change is possible. Paul's first application of this is to Timothy: he is to avoid those who are unworthy and purify himself. But if it works for Timothy it can work as well even for those caught in the devil's snare (2:26). Timothy's gentle manner of teaching is intended to change others, not conquer them. If he can demonstrate to them the "meekness and gentleness of Christ" (2 Cor 10:1), they may then have an example of the true servant of God to imitate: "God may perhaps grant that they will repent and come to know the truth, and they may escape from the snare of the devil" (2:26). Paul adds a final phrase, "after being captured by him to do his will." The syntax in Greek is very difficult, and opinions vary as to whether "his will" should refer to the devil or God. The choice of words, however, as well as the overall flow of the sentence, strongly suggest that the proper subject is God: God will give them repentance so that they can do his will. And in this context, "doing the will of God" is exactly what "the knowledge of the truth" is all about.

Paul provides Timothy with two sources for his teaching: Paul himself and the Scriptures (3:10–17). I will consider them in reverse order from their appearance in the text.

The statement concerning the role of the "sacred writings" in Timothy's own formation (3:14–17) is remarkable. We see first that Timothy is able to "continue in what you have learned and have firmly believed" (3:14), precisely because he *knows its origin*. Here again we encounter the importance of Timothy's childhood experiences of trust and loyalty (the "from whom" is in the plural!). The medium of his instruction was the Scripture. We can pass over here the part of the statement that ordinarily receives obsessive attention, namely "all Scripture is inspired by God", except to note that Paul is here obviously referring to Torah (no other "Scripture" was available to him) and is making what was in his understanding an inarguable and unremarkable claim. Clearly, Torah is God's word. God is Spirit. Therefore, Torah is "inspired of God." Paul adds nothing to this part of the statement, for nothing more is needed. When he states that Torah is inspired, he makes an attribution of authority. He does not state a theory of literary composition. For Paul Torah stands as God's Word and therefore as normative for all of human life. Those who cite this text today make the same claim. But for Paul Torah needed qualification by the new and surprising work of the Spirit in a crucified and raised Messiah. Torah was not a closed norm but one open to new meanings. Those who quote this text today sometimes do so in just the opposite sense: inspiration forbids new understanding. Frequently as well, the passage and its statement about inspiration are referred to the New Testament. This is clearly an error since Paul knew no New Testament. Sometimes it also happens that inspiration is taken as an accounting for Scripture's composition. This is less obviously but no less certainly an error. Saying that texts are inspired by God does not close a discussion but opens it. Such opinions are the more distressing because they have nothing to do with the point of Paul's statement and draw attention away from it, replacing Paul's pedagogic emphasis with a peculiarly contemporary preoccupation.

Much more fascinating and revealing are the *functions* Paul assigns to Torah. How can Torah "instruct you for salvation through faith in Christ Jesus" (3:15)? If we read only Paul's Letter to the Galatians we might suppose such a statement to be impossible, for in that place, the choice between Christ and Torah appears to be mutually exclusive. In Paul's overall understanding, however, Christ and Torah do not oppose each other but illuminate each other. The true "end" of Torah is to reveal the Messiah and God's way of making humans righteous by the response of faith (see Rom 3:21, 31; 10:4). More than that, Torah remains for Paul the indispensable framework for the Christian understanding of life before God. Not even the "law of love" can be grasped without reference to it (Rom 13:8–10; Gal 5:14). So Paul can say of the ascription of righteousness to Abraham in Genesis, "the words 'it was reckoned to him' were written not for his sake alone, but for ours also" (Rom 4:23). Likewise of the stories of the wilderness, "these things . . . were written down for our instruction, upon whom the end of the ages has come" (1 Cor 10:11), and of the psalms, "whatever was written in former days was written for

our instruction, that by steadfastness and by the encouragement of the scriptures we might have hope" (Rom 15:4). Torah
therefore has a direct didactic function even for those who
live by faith in a crucified Messiah.

Torah therefore is useful ("profitable," 3:16) in two ways.
First, it provides the Christian teacher and preacher with a
source of instruction. Its stories, sayings, and commandments are appropriate to the diverse moments and moods of
Christian pedagogy: teaching, reproof, correction. But the
second level of usefulness is even more important. The Scripture is not only a storehouse of proof texts. It is a whole world
of meaning which can form the Christian teacher himself or
herself: "that the man of God [which term includes "woman
of God"] may be complete, equipped for every good work"
(3:17), just as the vessel once cleansed and sanctified is "ready
for any good work" (2:21). As always in this letter, Paul's concern is not so much for the content of Timothy's teaching, as
his character and aptitude as a teacher.

Paul therefore provides Timothy with another source of information and imitation, his own example (3:10–12). Here is
a living text from which to learn. Paul reminds Timothy how
he had "observed" in Paul three levels of truth. The first was
the most external: "my teaching, my conduct, my aim in life."
The second level is that of the interior disposition corresponding to that teaching: "my faith, my love, my steadfastness." The third level brings us again to the immediate
concern Paul has for Timothy in this letter: "my persecutions,
my sufferings, what befell me at Antioch, at Iconium, and at
Lystra, what persecutions I endured" (3:11).

The preacher who truly preaches a crucified Messiah and
righteousness by faith preaches an affront to the measure-
ment of the world and will suffer persecution (see Gal 6:12–
14). The teacher who advances the paradoxical interpretation
of Torah based on the cross will have less "wisdom" than
scribes and sophists and will appear as foolish in their eyes
(see 1 Cor 1:18–25). The servant of God who approaches the
opposition with the gentleness and meekness of Christ will
also inevitably experience the sufferings of Christ, for such is
the way the world treats what it sees as foolishness and weakness (see 2 Cor 10–13).

Paul can offer Timothy therefore only two pieces of encouragement. The first is that his suffering will fit the pattern of God's work in the world, "all who desire to live a godly life in Christ Jesus will be persecuted (3:12). Notice the importance of "in Christ Jesus"; not every form of spirituality elicits opposition—the spirit of the crucified Messiah does, for it is an affront to every human pretense of power and self-interest. The world today as then is deeply offended by the proposition that rights are not supreme, that the self is not ultimate, that true life is found by sacrificing one's life for others. Timothy's suffering is therefore at least in this sense meaningful. Secondly, Paul can point to his own experience of liberation, "yet from them all the Lord rescued me" (3:11). The one working through Paul and Timothy is more powerful than the forces of evil. God is "able to guard [him] until that Day" (see 1:12–13). We can see how central is Paul's concern for Timothy's suffering when he closes this section with the instruction not only to fulfill his ministry and do the work of an evangelist, but also to "endure suffering" (4:5).

*   *   *   *   *

Already in the exposition of the text, I have tried to begin the process of questioning necessary for the text to speak to our lives. Here, I want to touch more directly on three aspects of this section of 2 Timothy which can be developed into sermons: the use of polemic, the role of virtue, and the gentle manner of Christian teaching.

The Use of Polemic.   We like to think of ourselves as irenic and ecumenic. We are enlightened and tolerant. We are therefore offended at Paul's use of polemic. Here is a direct challenge to some of our favorite presumptions. We have been indoctrinated with the understanding that "acceptance" means an almost infinite tolerance for difference, even—another offensive word—deviance from our own standards and the standards of our community. Truth is not important, only sincerity. Ideas are less important than feelings. People do not sin, they are only emotionally disturbed. So pervasive is this attitude that we can barely muster a societal consensus that

Hitler and Stalin were moral monsters. Some would like to withhold judgment on Idi Amin! We are uncomfortable calling killers of the innocent "terrorists," and collude in their deceptive camouflage of "freedom fighters." Closer to home, we are remarkably unwilling to risk calling the Hefners, Gucciones, and Flynts of this world what in fact they are, pornographers "depraved in conscience." We seem afraid to call the purveyors of psychobabble and auto-illumination what they in fact are, charlatans and deceivers, who "make a prey" of the gullible and whose "foolishness will soon be evident to all."

Within the Christian community, we have grown remarkably chary of the terms "heresy" and "orthodoxy." We think that a claim to hold the truth necessarily implies a stance of boastful and arrogant smugness. Won't the charge of heresy lead immediately to incivility and cruel inquisitions? Aren't we too progressive for all that? We have in fact grown so sensitive to offending others that our public prayers and declarations become exercises in lowest common denominator Christianity, addressed not to God but to the congregation for its edification in warm feelings about itself. We are so afraid of encroaching on anyone's "rights"—perhaps the most abused word in the English language over the past hundred years—or moral sensitivities that we cringe from plain speech altogether, failing to label as stupid and silly people who plainly are acting so, avoiding naming as small-minded and corrupt those who daily show themselves to be just that.

Paul's vigorous and straightforward use of polemical language should at least challenge these parts of our conventional and craven wisdom. To attack another's ideas is to take them seriously. Ideas do in fact matter. Feelings are excellent indicators of pleasure and pain, but they do not themselves reveal values. People do in fact live according to their ideas about the world. They will act consistently with their understanding of what constitutes success and failure. A racist interpretation of the world does lead logically to genocide. A Marxist view of history does lead logically to revolution and—if supplemented by Leninism—social engineering on a massive scale. A sexist perception of women does lead logically to sexual abuse. A Christian interpretation of life does demand selflessness and not the self-fulfillment parroted by self-actualization movements.

The ancient world was much smarter than ours in this area. We have become so psychologized that we fool ourselves about the primacy of feelings. In fact, ideas govern our actions and regulate our feeling! Some ideas therefore need attacking because they are dangerous. Some people need to be avoided and exposed because they peddle false ideas and corrupt others, particularly the uneducated and helpless.

We need to ask, in fact, whether our distaste for polemic really derives from a spirit of tolerance (the attitude Paul calls "longsuffering"), and Christian acceptance, or from a distressing decline in our convictions concerning the truth. The refusal to take truth seriously *is* a "corruption of the mind." Not all truths are relative, after all. The transposition of relativity from theoretical physics to the realm of values is one of the outrageous fallacies of the twentieth century. The truth we speak of in the Christian community furthermore is not that of abstraction but of existence. It is not excessive to fight for genuine virtue over camouflaged vice. The unwillingness or incapacity to enter this battle is not a sign of moral health, but a warning signal of moral corruption.

The Place of Virtues. My remarks above lead rather naturally to this second scandalous aspect of 2 Timothy: that morals matter. As I mentioned earlier, polemic against an opponent's morals works only if we agree that bad ideas lead to bad morals. By condemning the morals, we rule the ideas out of court as well.

Once again, however, there is an element in the theological atmosphere which regards virtue and vice as irrelevant to the life of faith. When Paul tells Timothy to "aim at righteousness, faith, love, and peace, along with those who call upon the Lord from a pure heart" (2:22), some commentators grow apologetic, as though this list of virtues represented a significant corruption of the pure gospel preached by Paul. In that version, of course, "righteousness" is only God's forensic declaration concerning humans. "Faith" is an authentic existential decision. "Love" is an unequivocal self-disposition for the other. "Peace" is the covenantal condition established between God and humans by the reconciling work of Christ. To think of these "theological" realities as human qualities or virtues implies that the human response to reality may be more than a once for all "existential decision," may even involve thinking about anthropology or human nature. In the eyes of some, that sort of thinking is actually blasphemous.

But so narrow a reading even of Paul's unquestioned letters is achieved only by eliminating important evidence. Paul is perfectly capable elsewhere of speaking about "righteousness" as though it were a virtue (see Rom 6:13, 19, and especially 14:17). He can speak of "pursuing" peace (Rom 14:19) and "pursuing" love (1 Cor 14:1). He can speak of faith as one quality among others (1 Cor 13:13), which can grow (2 Cor 10:15) and can be expressed as a fruit of the Spirit (Gal 5:22). The theological position that demands that faith be nothing else than an existential decision is itself notoriously inept at translating that decision into a consistent pattern of life.

Actually, just as the theological response of faith does not destroy but builds on the human experiences of trust and loyalty, so also do the virtues represent (on the other side) the habituated interiorization of the attitudes consonant with faith in God. The genuine Christian can be described in terms of a definite "character." Life is not simply a matter of random and radical "decisions," one unconnected to another. Life is, rather, the slowly evolving creation of patterns by our human freedom. We create character by our choices, and our character in turn directs our subsequent choices. The importance of this truth is clear. If the dominant pattern of people's lives is self-centered, hostile, and deceitful, they cannot be said to be living according to "the truth" of the gospel, whatever their protestations to the contrary. Likewise, those whose lives form patterns of peace, love, fidelity, and justice reveal precisely the truth of that "good news" from God. It is therefore a critical aspect of Christian discernment of the Spirit to look at such patterns: what are our habits? It is a vital element in Christian education to form such patterns. The virtues enable and facilitate our choices of the good.

The Gentle Teacher. In light of my fondness for polemic, it is all the more important that I emphasize this most surprising aspect of Paul's vision of the ideal Christian teacher. Despite his attacks on the crass ideas and shoddy morals of the opponents, Paul nowhere encourages Timothy to treat them harshly. He is not to avoid them, only their ideas, morals, and methods. In fact, he is to act as their *teacher.* As such, he is to be "apt," that is, he is to fit his mode of discourse to their needs. When he rebukes, corrects, or encourages, it is not because of his moods or their desires but because of their needs. Above all, he is to be longsuffering and gentle. The exact opposite of a sectarian attitude is here advocated. Timothy is to work ceaselessly for their change. He is to try to convince them. Timothy remains within the society even when its "itching ears" reject him. He does not seek to demolish the opposition or even silence it. His is a gentle persuasion. This is truly a noble and difficult ideal: to hate the sin but not the sinner, to take ideas seriously but human lives even more so, to suffer the indignity of involvement and commitment even when it is least desired by others.

Paul the Model of Suffering (4:6–22)

At first sight the final section of 2 Timothy appears to consist only in autobiographical remarks and short practical commands. But the same literary intention which shaped the rest of the letter is at work here as well. In these final words, Paul presents himself once more to Timothy as the model of one who suffers for the Lord in hope.

The literary fashioning is evident at once from the way Paul joins together the first of his personal statements and his solemn charge to Timothy with the connective, "for" (4:6). Timothy is to endure suffering and fulfill his ministry *because* Paul is now at the point of death. Two points are implied by this connection. The first is that Timothy must carry on the work since Paul will no longer be able to. The second is that Timothy is to be faithful to the end in the manner Paul is now showing him.

All of Paul's language in 4:6–8 points to the immediacy of his death. He is "already" being sacrificed and the time of his departure (or "release") is here (4:6). He had used this language of sacrifice also in Philippians, but there it was in the form of a conditional, "if I am spent in sacrifice" (Phil 2:17, author's translation). Here it is a present reality almost completed. His life follows the trajectory of the Messiah's as he endures all things "for the sake of the elect" (2 Tim 2:10). Paul also returns to the image of the athlete introduced in 2:5. He had told Timothy that the athlete must compete by the rules if he wishes to be crowned. Now he states confidently, "I have fought a noble fight, I have run the race" (author's translation). He adds also a final phrase which explicates how he had "played by the rules" of his Christian identity: "I have kept the faith" (4:7). The phrase could in this context equally well be translated, "I have remained loyal," for this is exactly what Paul has been encouraging Timothy to do. Because Paul has so struggled, he is certain that he will be given the "crown of righteousness." The phrase can be read several ways. This could be the crown given him as a reward for *his* righteousness. Or it could be the crown given him which consists in "righteousness," that is, in his being declared righteous. It does not after all matter, for the significant thing is that it is rewarded by the "righteous judge," and therein lies his confidence: Paul has earlier averred, "he cannot deny himself" (2:13). Paul makes sure that Timothy does not miss the point, for he immediately generalizes his expectation. The just judge will give this crown also to "all those who have loved his coming" (4:8, author's translation). The "struggle" side of the athlete's example was held before Timothy in 2:5; here the "reward" side is stressed. If Timothy holds on, he too will be rewarded.

A similar paraenetic purpose is served by Paul's second long statement in 2:16–18. He acknowledges that nobody stayed with him in his first defense—they all abandoned him (4:16). Paul, in a word, faces circumstances far more severe than those faced by Timothy. Yet he does not lose courage. Why? "The Lord stood by me and gave me strength to proclaim the message fully, that all the Gentiles might hear it" (4:17). Paul was "strengthened" by the presence of the Lord even though he was abandoned by people, and he was able to "fulfill his ministry" to the Gentiles. The point could hardly be missed by Timothy, who has been repeatedly told that he also had received a spirit of power (1:7), that the Lord was powerful to preserve him (1:12), and that he should "grow strong" in the grace of Christ Jesus (2:1). Once again, Paul holds out the possibility of release. He was "rescued from the lion's mouth" at the first defense (4:17) as he had been in all his previous sufferings (3:11). And this should give Timothy some encouragement. Paul's deeper hope, however, is not based in the vagaries of the judicial system: "The Lord will rescue me from every evil [deed] and save me for his heavenly kingdom. To him be the glory for ever and ever. Amen" (4:18). For Paul the horizon of hope is not simply this life with its transitory success and failure. In an earlier letter he had mocked such a closed horizon: "If for this life only we have hoped in Christ, we are of all men most to be pitied," and again, . . . "if the dead are not raised, 'let us eat and drink, for tomorrow we die'" (1 Cor 15:19, 32). If "liberation" is only within the horizon of human potential, then suffering is meaningless. But, in fact, Paul lives and dies in the sight of one who is a "master" (2:21) and a "just judge" (4:8). He is convinced that the one who died for all will also come "to judge the living and the dead" (4:1). He is certain that "on that Day" (1:12, 18; 4:8) he will be adequately rewarded for his life and death in the service of Jesus and the elect; not with an athlete's crown, but with a share in "his heavenly kingdom," that is (if we unpack the argot of "heaven"), a kingdom that absolutely transcends all human capacities and cravings because it is of God. Paul is confident of this because, as he has already told Timothy, "If we have died with him, we shall also live with him; if we endure, we shall also reign with him" (2:11–12). For Paul, this "saying is sure" (2:11).

Despite this confident vision of what awaits him at his death, Paul by no means neglects the very human dimensions of his situation. Throughout the letter, as we have seen, he has been urging Timothy to fight this good fight with and for him. Even now, the battle continues against Alexander the coppersmith, "who greatly resists our words" and against whom, therefore, Timothy must "guard himself" (4:15, author's translation). But Paul also wants Timothy to be *with him* in his final days. He had earlier reminded Timothy of how Onesiphorus had "not been ashamed of my chains" when he had visited and refreshed Paul in prison (1:15–17). Now, Paul wants Timothy to join him. His need is all the greater since he had either sent off, or been abandoned by, nearly all his co-workers, save Luke. As we read 4:9–21 carefully, we see that Paul has once more alternated news about himself and others with a series of direct commands to Timothy (4:9, 11, 13, 15, 19, 21). When we isolate these short commands, Paul's overwhelming desire to be joined by Timothy is manifest: "do your best to come to me soon" (4:9); "Bring [Mark] with you" (4:11); "bring ... the books, and ... parchments" (4:13); "Greet Prisca and Aquila, and the household of Onesiphorus"—a subtle touch (4:19); "Do your best to come before winter" (4:21).

At the beginning of this letter, Paul laid great emphasis on the network of faith and loyalty which had shaped the character of Timothy. At the end of the letter, he calls for the same loyalty to be shown him. He too needs the support of the one he taught, as he lives out the most painful final lesson of the Christian teacher.

* * * * *

Two features of this final section of 2 Timothy call out for some comment. Both have to do with the uses of religious language.

The Language of Faith. We cannot miss how Paul uses a language deeply colored by religious symbols, even when speaking about matters most personal. He also, it is true, uses the language of the Olympic Games, but in his culture even those allusions were filled with residual religious content: the image of the athlete finishing his course evoked the memory of apotheosized heroes like Heracles. Mostly, however, Paul uses the language of Torah and of the nascent Christian tradition. He does not say he is lonely, but that he has "been abandoned." He does not hope that the emperor will release him but that "the Lord will rescue me." He does not say, "I have tried hard" but "I have kept the faith."

To some extent, just such language keeps us at a distance from the real and poigant human situation Paul describes. All the centuries of Christian use and abuse of such language

have made his appear not fresh but banal. Many of us today
recoil at the use of "pious talk." We associate it with hypocrisy
or self-alienation. People use religious language to cover up
their more sinister motives. Or people use religious language
because they are out of touch with their real motives (feelings). A large part of our "pastoral counseling," therefore,
often consists in a kind of linguistic therapy. By using the her-
meneutics of suspicion, we "translate" the pious talk used by
ourselves and others, in an attempt to discover what we
"really" mean.

This reactive stage has now gone on long enough that we
as a religious community face the opposite peril. So critical
have we become of our language and symbolic system and so
embarrassed by using it in direct discourse, that it is in danger of becoming precisely a dead language. It has become so,
interestingly, most of all among those who ought to be the
grammarians of the faith, theologians and pastors. In some
cases, these "religious professionals" have become the most
cynical in their employment of the symbols of faith. Like the
stereotypes of the hypocritical monks of old who preached
chastity but practiced fornication, these ministers use the
language of faith in the pulpit, but parody it in private. Words
like "grace" or "providence" or "God's will" are spoken by the
sophisticated pastor only within inverted commas, or with
ironically raised eyebrows. Real language cannot sustain
such a schizophrenic division.

There are two simplistic solutions. The first is simply to
return to the language of Paul and the Gospels, forcing our
experience and perceptions to match it. But of course that is
impossible. We have come too far. It truly is no longer simply
"our language." The other option is to abandon the language
of faith altogether in favor of another linguistic system, say
that of psychotherapy. This option has in fact been chosen by
many, as is evident from a generous selection of sermons and
most "pastoral counseling." But this option is still more destructive than the first, for it fundamentally changes our
identity.

We need reminding that language does not only describe
reality, it also in the most basic way constitutes reality. There
is a real difference between a "gut feeling," or even a "guilt

feeling," and "conscience." There is a distance between "error,"
or "failure," or "inadequacy," and "sin." A great chasm separates "I'm OK you're OK," and "the Grace of God in Jesus
Christ." Because we use the symbols and stories of our tradition we are part of that tradition, and not some other. Because we use this language *together* we are a people. Because
we *use* this language, we perceive our lives in a different way
than if we used another language. We cannot in promethean
fashion simply start over. Symbols cannot be taken on and off
like T-shirts.

Then what is our proper course? The solution lies not at the
theoretical level, but at the level of practical application and
usage. It is not a simple solution but a complex one. It is
not effected by fiat but by the friction of hard encounters. It
demands the willingness of pastors and preachers and
theologians and laypeople to exercise the asceticism of atten-
tiveness in their use of language. We must together begin
again to "try on" the symbols and stories from our shared
past, as we speak of the significant experiences of our lives, to
see how they fit our experience and how our experience fits
them. And as in all fittings, we need to be aware of two quite
separate possibilities. The clothes sometimes may not fit because they are too small or too large. On the other hand, they
may not fit because we have become too meager, or perhaps
too flabby.

The Language of Liberation.   Here is a case in point. In this
final section of the letter, Paul uses the language of liberation.
The Lord "rescued him" from every persecution earlier in his
career (3:11). He was "rescued" at his first defense "from the
lion's mouth" (4:17). And he knows that "The Lord will rescue
me from every evil deed and save me for his heavenly kingdom" (4:18). The language of "rescuing" and "saving" is the
language of liberation.

The language of liberation is extremely popular in some
versions of theology today. A whole subcategory of theological
discourse (use of the language of faith) has termed itself "liberation theology." But when we ask of this discourse what
"liberation" means, the answer is put in terms of various "ac-
tualizations" of human potential. People are freed, we are

told, from various "oppressions" consisting in conditions of poverty, discrimination, ignorance, and so forth. How are they freed? They can begin to realize their "full potential" as human beings. In some circles this is virtually identified as the essence of the gospel.

I would suggest that Paul has something else in mind when he uses the language of "liberation." He does not seem to have much of a concept of "human potential" as an absolute good or inalienable category. In fact, he seems to find suffering for others not as something to be freed from but something to be freed for. In the shortest terms, he expresses liberation this way: the Lord will rescue him from "every evil deed" and will save him "for his heavenly kingdom."

If our language of faith is to be both alive and consistent with its intrinsic grammar, we must begin to ask certain hard questions about the easy equation between what the texts say and what we would like to see happen. Is there a connection between Paul's understanding of liberation, and that purveyed in liberation theology? Are they even compatible? More on this, later.

1 TIMOTHY

How to Live in God's Household
Introduction

The situation presupposed by 1 Timothy is far less specifically detailed than the one in 2 Timothy. In that letter, Paul wrote from prison, whereas here he is ostensibly traveling on mission. He has left the city of Ephesus in Asia Minor to go to Macedonia, leaving Timothy in Ephesus (1:3). Paul expects to return shortly (3:14; 4:13), although he might be delayed (3:15). This is all we learn of Paul or his plans.

Ephesus was a city well known to Paul and very much involved with his mission (see Acts 18:18–21, 24–28; 19:8–20), although he does not seem to have founded the church (or churches) there. It was to the elders of the Ephesian church that Paul made his farewell speech before departing to Jerusalem and eventual imprisonment (Acts 20:17–38). In the speech also, he calls the elders "overseers" (Acts 20:28), revealing the same fluidity in terminology for church officials as we find in 1 Timothy and Titus.

Timothy associated with Paul throughout this period of Ephesian ministry, acting as his emissary (see Acts 19:22; 20:4; 1 Cor 4:17; 16:10; 2 Cor 1:1, 19) But although Acts tells us that Paul sent Timothy and Erastus to Macedonia in preparation for one of his own trips there (Acts 19:22), it never mentions Paul leaving Timothy in charge of Ephesus while he himself went to Macedonia. Acts, of course, omits or generalizes other trips made by Paul (see, for example, 2 Cor 2:1; 13:1; Acts 18:23). Nothing in the text prevents our placing the letter in the period of Paul's active Aegean ministry. Indeed, it could even have been written from a captivity which Paul expected to end shortly, although there is certainly no positive evidence for that. On the other hand, a pseudepigrapher—one writing under Paul's name—would seem to have had good information both from Acts and from the Corinthian letters (see the correlation on the role and character of Timothy in 1 Cor 4:17; 16:10–11; and 1 Tim 4:12) and yet been unable to get Paul's itinerary precisely correct.

In any case, Timothy's role during the time of Paul's absence is clear. He is to function as Paul's representative to this local community (see also 1 Cor 4:17; Phil 2:19–23). Specifically, Paul wants him to deal with the problems of deviant teaching (1:3; 4:6) and community structures. He is not appointed by Paul as head of the local church but retains his role as delegate. He is to teach and command (4:11) in Paul's absence, seeing in particular to the "reading, preaching, and teaching" (4:13). If we read carefully, we see that Timothy is by no means establishing new structures and procedures. Rather, he is responding to problems arising from structures already in place. Even if all this is fictional, it is good to get the fiction straight: 1 Timothy does not invent a church order. Timothy is required instead to solve difficulties posed by existing procedures, particularly when they are being tested by "certain persons" in the community who teach "other doctrine."

The literary character of 1 Timothy matches the situation envisaged. The letter lacks the tight and coherent literary structure of 2 Timothy. Its Greek style and vocabulary are also further along that line of distinctiveness which is usually termed "un-pauline." It is difficult to determine how much of the distinctive style is due to the special purpose and subject matter of the letter; I tend to attribute more to these factors than other readers do.

Elements of the personal paraenetic letter such as we found them in 2 Timothy are also present here: Paul presents himself as a model, though in quite a different manner (1 Tim 1:16). On the other hand, Timothy is now explicitly told to be a "model" for the church both in speech and conduct (4:12, 15). We can even detect some antithetical arrangement of polemic against the opponents set out as contrast to the practice Timothy should follow (see 1:3–11, 18–20; 4:6–16; 6:3–16, 20–21). Timothy is to "avoid" and "shun" the practices of the opponents (4:7; 6:11, 20). As in 2 Timothy as well, the opponents are slandered with more or less stereotyped charges. In fact, if we were to pull out only those sections of 1 Timothy which deal with the delegate and his performance, we should have just the sort of personal paraenetic letter that we found in 2 Timothy.

In 1 Timothy, however, these elements are subordinated in two significant ways, which give the letter its special character. First, the opponents are not only slandered, they are also theologically rebutted. Paul reminds Timothy of the proper understanding of the issues controverted by the opponents (1:8–11; 4:3–5, 8–10; 6:6–10). In contrast to 2 Timothy, then, Paul is as much concerned here with the *content* of his delegate's teaching as he is with his capacities and character. This distinctive touch is expressed well by 1 Tim 4:16: "Take heed to yourself and to your teaching; hold to that, for by so doing, you will save both yourself and your hearers."

Second, Paul gives Timothy specific directives for the resolution of community difficulties. Timothy is to both "command and teach these things" (4:11). The term "command" in both its verbal and substantive forms (*parangello, parangelia*) occurs more often here than in any other Pauline letter (1:3, 5, 18; 4:11; 5:7; 6:13, 17), although Paul uses it often enough elsewhere, and in much the same sort of way (see 1 Thess 4:2, 11; 2 Thess 3:4, 6, 10, 12; 1 Cor 7:10; 11:17). These commands are briefly encapsulated in the verse which many take as the theme of the whole letter: "how one ought to behave in the household of God" (3:15).

Actually, the directives have a much more random and *ad hoc* character than at first may appear; we are yet a long way from the *Apostolic Constitutions*. Still, these parts of the letter fall into separate thematic discussions: matters of worship (2:1–15), qualifications for local leadership (3:1–13), care of widows (5:3–16), payment and other problems of elders (5:17–22), slaves and masters (6:1–2), and the rich (6:17–19).

It will perhaps be noticed that these sections are not only disconnected from each other but also alternate with the sections dealing with Timothy's personal duties and conflicts with the opposition. It is almost as though the form of the personal paraenetic letter as we find it in 2 Timothy has been opened up to provide room for the specific instructions in 1 Timothy, without any real resolution of the literary tensions thereby created.

* * * * *

Contemporary readers of 1 Timothy have serious interpretive difficulties with which to contend. Most of them center on the "command" character of this text. Commands by their nature obviously expect obedience. The more practical, specific, and particular a command, however, the more difficult it is to execute, at least if the command goes beyond the "insert tab *a* into slot *a*" variety, to matters of social arrangements. The fact that these particular commands have (quite unintentionally) found their way into a canonical collection of "Scripture," so that their instructions become at once generalized and sacralized, has not made matters easier. Nor has the nearly two thousand years' distance between the social structures presupposed by those commands and our own, a period of time filled moreover with successive layers of interpretation.

The historical intention of the commands is not terribly difficult to reconstruct. Some aspects of the Ephesian situation remain obscure but not so much that the basic problems and Pauline responses cannot be understood. The difficulties rather lie in translating such commands into meaningful messages for the contemporary church. This is made more problematic still by the fact that some of these commands have attached to them a religious warrant, as in the case of women keeping silent in the church (2:11–15). If we assent to the command, do we need also assent to its justification? Can we assent to the justification without literally fulfilling the command? Can we ignore both? The problem is scarcely isolated in this passage or even this letter; it is only more obvious here because of the crisp nature of the commands. If we have no fear of the angels in worship, for example, or do not regard it as shameful for women to have their hair cut short, does this mean we should *not* have women veiled in church (1 Cor 11)? If we do not in fact have people baptized in behalf of the deceased—as, I think, none of us do—(1 Cor 15:29), does that necessarily weaken our convictions concerning the resurrection of the dead? If we disagree that Eve was seduced but not Adam (1 Tim 2:14) should this affect our practice concerning women's role in ministry?

One simple option is to decide that the commands and reasons alike made sense only for the historical situation and have no further applicability today. This is tempting not only for the sake of clarity but also because some aspects both of the commands and of the reasons remain a stumbling block to our own perceptions. Certainly this is so in the case of women's role in the assembly. Unfortunately, once we reduce writings simply to their historical significance, we also lose something equally important. We close off the possibility of their continuing to speak to and challenge our own age and ages other than our own, as well as to places and circumstances other than our own, in ways we cannot predict. If we do not read 1 Tim 2:8–15, why should we read 1 Tim 2:4, where Paul says, "God wills the salvation of all people"?

Another simple option is to follow the commands literally and try to force our lives into their frame. This option gains in mechanical obedience but perhaps not in true fidelity. Whether acknowledged or not, such attempts are always selective in what they take seriously and what they do not. Our women do not speak in the assembly, for example, but they do wear jewelry. But the text forbids both. On the other hand, if we allow one, why not the other? Likewise, we may organize our community into a system of elders, and even follow 1 Timothy in their manner of payment, but do we also follow it in the matter of charges against them? No contemporary church so lives within the social structure of the Ephesian church that Paul's commands can be followed without selection and interpretation.

A third (more complex) option is to take both the canonical text and our own experience of God seriously and to bring them into a continuing and honest confrontation, allowing neither to dictate absolutely to the other, but allowing each to inform and shape the other. In this option, neither our experience nor the text is accepted or rejected without critical reflection. In this option, there is the recognition that we live as community at all only because we continue to be shaped by these normative texts; but there is also the recognition that these texts live at all only because the experience of God's spirit enables the community to engage them always in new and surprising ways, not with the rigid submission of slaves, but with the joyful fidelity of children. Such is not an easy process, and it is certainly risk-filled. It is particularly avoided by those who for whatever reason and from whatever direction, prefer an authoritative and univocal meaning to one which authorizes and energizes God's people. For that very reason, it is a process most necessary for the church today.

Conscience and Law (1:1–20)

As so often in Paul's letters, we gain an impression of the situation and of Paul's intentions from the very beginning. In the greeting, Paul says he is an apostle "by *command* of God our savior" (1:1, author's italics), and this note of commandment runs all through the letter as Paul in turn commits this charge to Timothy (1:18). More strikingly, the letter lacks an opening thanksgiving section. In only one other Pauline letter (if we exclude Titus) does Paul not begin with a prayer of thanksgiving or blessing, and that is the thunderous *thaumazo* ("I am astonished") of Gal 1:6, when his outrage over the abandonment of the gospel demanded explosive expression. No such outburst here, but Paul's immediate attention to the problem of opposing teachers (1:3–12, 18–20) indicates the seriousness of the problem they pose. Only after he has given some initial directives concerning them can he begin to deal with the problems arising from the church's common life.

Who were these opponents, and what were they teaching? As in every attempt to identify Paul's opposition, there are obvious difficulties. Should we join the evidence here to what we learned in 2 Timothy or treat each letter separately? Should we try to attach the description here to historical parties about which we have other (though often equally fuzzy)

information? Making up our mind about our main task helps
clarify these decisions. If our main goal is understanding the
text in its literary integrity rather than historical reconstruction, then it is appropriate to take as sufficient the information given only in this letter, for the point is not who these
people really were, but how Paul understood them and how
his view of them shaped his presentation.

That said, however, we cannot altogether avoid making one
connection to 2 Timothy, for there is mention of a Hymenaeus
and Alexander in 1 Tim 1:20, who (apparently) also appear as
members of Paul's opposition in 2 Tim 2:17 and 4:14. Can we
then go further and identify the other doctrine mentioned in
1 Tim 1:3 with their claim that the resurrection had already
come, in 2 Tim 2:17? Possibly, though there is no real evidence of that teaching in 1 Timothy, nor is it clear how it
would help us understand the claims that are being advanced
in this letter. Better to restrict ourselves altogether to 1 Timothy and see what sense we can make of the information it
gives us.

The opponents were members of the community, for Paul
assumes that they lie within Timothy's "charge" (1:3), and
that he himself can give directions concerning them (1:20). It
is clear as well that they represent an intellectual elite. They
want to be regarded as "teachers" of some sort. Timothy's
problem, then, is not simply moral failure or misunderstand-
ing among the common people but the competing claims of
rival teachers.

We are not surprised to find them characterized as those
who "have made shipwreck of their faith" (1:19), who engage
in "vain discussions" (1:6), or who promote "speculations"
(1:4). All this falls into the category of stereotyped polemic.
Not much more is learned by Paul saying that they involve
themselves in "myths and endless genealogies" (1:4) even
though he repeats the charge (4:7). Too many people those
days did that sort of thing. More informative, however, is the
way Paul opposes that activity to the *oikonomia theou* (1:4).
This is a difficult phrase, and the RSV's "divine training" is
probably much too narrow. At the least it means, "God's way
of ordering things," and probably refers here, as elsewhere in
Paul, to God's way of saving humans through faith in the Mes-

siah (see Col 1:25; Eph 1:10; 3:2, 9). Even more specifically opposed to this "divine dispensation" is their wanting to be "teachers of the law" (1:7). This seems to be their chief identifying feature, even if its meaning is obscure, not least because the only other NT occurrences of the term "teachers of the law" refer to associates of the Pharisees (Luke 5:17 and Acts 5:34). Perhaps the context and Paul's argument can help us figure out what these Christian teachers were up to.

They were intellectuals who claimed to have "knowledge" (6:20) enabling them to arbitrate the moral behavior of others on the basis of "the Law." Paul says that their project is vitiated by their being "without understanding either what they are saying or the things about which they make assertions" (1:7). We are not sure at this point what these assertions might entail. It is intriguing, however, that Paul twice places their pretensions in direct opposition to "faith and a good conscience" (1:5, 19). They have Paul says, rejected both. The terms "faith" and "conscience" here are often understood as the sort of purely formal language typical of the Pastorals' routinization of Paul's theological vocabulary. Because of the way Paul places just these terms over against the claims of the opposing teachers, however, a second and closer look appears worthwhile.

We know that Paul speaks elsewhere of "conscience" (*syneidesis*) as a moral consciousness on the basis of which, or by which, a person chooses to act or not to act in a certain fashion (see, for example, Rom 2:15; 1 Cor 8:7–12; 10:25–29). It is an internal, reflective, capacity for decision-making. Like the "heart" of the biblical tradition, Paul uses "conscience" as a way of referring to the conscious disposition of human freedom. He can therefore invoke his "conscience" as a "witness" to himself and his integrity (Rom 9:1; 2 Cor 1:12) and can appeal to the same capacity in others (see 2 Cor 4:2; 5:11). Paul can also use the term "faith" similarly as an obedient response to God that is not fully regulated by "Law" even though it may be witnessed to by "Law and Prophets" (see Rom 3:21–31).

Now we find people who reject the principles of "faith" and "conscience" in favor of a certain understanding of "law." What can this mean? They do not seem to be making soteriological claims for the law, and so we are not dealing with the Torah/Christ conflict. But as we read through the letter, two things about the opponents impress us. First, they are never charged by Paul with immorality of the grosser sort. The only traditional vice attributed to them is love of money (1 Tim 6:5). Otherwise, their vices are intellectual, not moral. Second, they advance a rigorist form of morality. They forbid marriage and certain foods (4:3–4) and demand physical asceticism (4:8).

By putting this information together we arrive at a reasonable picture: these would-be teachers of the law put aside the traditional Pauline emphasis on the discernment of faith and conscience within the community as guides to proper moral behavior and replace them with a code morality based on "Law"—in all likelihood based on a rigorist reading of Torah. Paul is therefore in the delicate position of offering "commandments" concerning church affairs, while at the same time maintaining the principles of faith and conscience as the fundamental guides to moral behavior.

Paul responds vigorously to the threat. He first exercises his own authority, by ordering Alexander and Hymenaeus to be delivered "to Satan that they may learn not to blaspheme" (1:20). We know from Paul's admonition to excommunicate the incestuous man of Corinth that he was not opposed to strong action taken against deviance in the community when it touched on a central point of identity or integrity (1 Cor 5:1–5). In the Corinthian case, the man was handed over to Satan for "the destruction of the flesh, that his spirit may be saved in the day of the Lord Jesus" (1 Cor 5:5). The problem to be cured there had to do precisely with the "flesh" in the narrowest sense, that is, sexual derangement. In the case of 1 Tim 1:20, the deviance is doctrinal. It is therefore appropriate that the excommunication is to accomplish a change of mind, "so that they may be *educated* not to blaspheme" (author's translation).

Paul's second response is to exhort his delegate to "wage the good warfare" against the opposition (1:18). Paul uses again the image of the teacher as soldier which he employs also in 2 Tim 2:4 and 1 Cor 9:6, and thereby touches on a favorite image for his ministry: a battle for good against spiritual forces (see 2 Cor 10:3–6; Eph 6:10–17). Timothy carries the battle to the opponents first of all by forbidding this "other teaching" (1:3). But he must also present to the people the proper understanding (4:11–12); so Paul reminds him of his prophetic appointment (1:18) and of the essence of God's ordering (1:4) which has as its goal (*telos* 1:5) a "pure heart and a good conscience and sincere faith" (1:5, 19).

Third, Paul clarifies for his delegate the proper perception of "the law" which the opponents seek to propound. He begins with a thoroughly typical characterization of Torah: "we know that the law is good" (or: "noble," *kalos*, 1:8), a statement which echoes "we know that the law is spiritual" (Rom 7:14) and "the law is holy, and the commandment is holy and just and good" (*agathos*, Rom 7:12). But in this place Paul adds, "if one uses it lawfully (*nomimos*). This at first strikes us as odd: how can Torah be used by Christians "lawfully"— isn't the law, according to Paul, to be normed not by itself but by faith in the Messiah (see Rom 10:4)? Yes, and that is what Paul means here as well. His whole statement is governed by its concluding phrase, in accordance with [that is, "normed by"] the glorious gospel of the blessed God with which I have been entrusted" (1:11).

The term "lawfully," then, should be seen as one of Paul's paradoxical puns, similar to "the law of Christ" (Gal 6:2) or "the law of faith" (Rom 3:27, author's translation). Paul means by it here exactly what he meant in 2 Tim 2:5 when he said that an athlete would be crowned only if he competed "lawfully" (*nomimos*)—that is, "properly," or "according to the governing rules." So when Paul speaks here of "using the law lawfully" he means precisely the law as normed by the gospel.

What, then, is the proper function of the law in light of the gospel? Paul introduces this with the phrase, "understanding this" (1:9) which provides a neat contrast to the pretentious ignorance of the opponents (1:7). Theirs is only a "falsely called knowledge" (6:20). The proper understanding is given by the play on another Greek verb, this time the verb *keimai*. In its first occurrence, it has the meaning "laid down for" (as the RSV has it); that is, "apply to." In the second use, it is joined to the prefix *anti-* to form *antikeitai*, "stand opposed to." The law, we are to understand, does not "apply" to the "righteous person." It "applies" instead to those who perform all the actions which are "opposed to" the sound teaching of the gospel. We need not pause over all the categories of sin Paul lists here, except to note the general resemblance to the equally extensive vice list in Rom 1:29–31. More important is determining how Paul can say that the Torah, which is good, does not "apply to the righteous."

There is no question that Paul speaks here of "the law" not as revelation or wisdom (the broader senses of "Torah") but in the narrow sense of "commandment" (*mitzvah, entole*). In the broader sense of Torah, the law could point to the Messiah and the principle of righteousness by faith (Rom 3:21). But in the narrower sense of "commandment," Paul agrees here with his stand in Rom 7:7–11. The commandment reveals and condemns sin but cannot fundamentally effect freedom from it. "The righteous person" in contrast, is able to live on the basis of the "dispensation of God," that is by the "pure heart, good conscience and sincere faith" made possible by the gift of God in Christ. For one made righteous, the commandments provide at best a minimal guidance—but they no longer either condemn or adequately direct behavior—that comes from the Spirit (see Rom 8:1–17). For the "teachers of law" to abandon these interior norms for a code of behavior means in effect to deny the reality of the gift, and this, for Paul, means to "shipwreck" their faith (1:19, see also Gal 5:4).

The mention of the "glorious gospel" reminds Paul of his own appointment as an apostle, "with which I have been entrusted" (1:11), which leads him in turn to a thanksgiving period focusing entirely on his conversion and call to be an apostle. This is not only a thoroughly Pauline move (see 1 Cor 15:1–11; Rom 1:1–6; Gal 1:11–15), but its specific rhetorical function here helps us appreciate both the solidity and subtlety of Paul's argument. The recitation of his past is by no means random: it is the key to the whole presentation in this first chapter. Paul claims that he had received mercy for this very reason: "that in me, as the foremost, Jesus Christ might display his perfect patience for an example to those who were to believe in him for eternal life" (1:16). Three things in this statement deserve emphasis: first, Paul is an example to those who would "believe in Christ," that is, those who have "faith" (*pisteuontes*). Second, he is an example in his own life of God's effective mercy that can change a person from one state to another. Third, he is such an example in a primordial way, as the "foremost" (*protos*), one might even translate, "prototypically." How do these points work in Paul's argument? They make him stand as the prime example of the efficacy of "the gospel." Paul declares this saying is sure: "Christ Jesus came into the world to save sinners" (1:15). The resemblance of this declaration to Jesus' self-designation of his mission in the synoptic tradition is striking (see Luke 19:10). But Paul's point is directly made: before his conversion he was also the "first" (*protos*) of sinners. Out of ignorance, he acted faithlessly and "blasphemed" in his persecution of the church (1:13–14). Why did Paul persecute the church? As he tells us in Galatians, it was because he was "zealous for the law" and could not recognize Jesus as the Christ precisely because he was by his manner of death cursed by Torah (Gal 1:13–14; 3:10–13). Paul therefore illustrates in his own experience how God's mercy is powerful to change people from faithlessness (1:13) to faith (1:12). The gift of the Lord "overflowed . . . with the faith and love" in his calling (1:14).

The rhetorical point is therefore simple. Paul stands as the prime example of the dispensation of God since it was by pure gift that he was changed and empowered (1:12) to live a life of faith and love. Those who therefore want to place Christian life again under the absolute framework of the law are in effect also blaspheming (see 1:20), for they do not recognize the reality of God's gift and how it has effected a change in people, so that they can live with a pure heart, good conscience, and sincere faith. They are truly ignorant of the matters they purport to teach.

*   *   *   *   *

This opening section of 1 Timothy not only provides us with a glimpse of a first generational struggle between an elitist attempt to regulate morals by law and the apostle's appeal to the *oikonomia* of God but also an opportunity to reflect over

our own instincts when confronted by the same options.
Paul's thoughts here provide us with seeds for sermons.

The Appeal to Experience. Contemporary theologians have,
with considerable delight, rediscovered *narrative* as a theological tool. If the category remains only another theological
abstraction, not much is gained. But if the true significance
of story-telling in the community of faith is realized, then theology itself can be renewed. When Paul tells the story of his
conversion and proposes it as an example to others, he is in
effect making an appeal to *experience.* He reminds us that
Christianity is not simply a set of convictions, a code of behavior, or an interpretation of the world. It is a response to a
certain kind of experience. That experience, furthermore,
continues in the world. Paul suggests that as the mercy of
God was shown him, so is it also to others. This means that
we meet the living God in the human experience of ourselves
and others. Only as these are raised to the level of *narrative,*
however, only insofar as we learn to perceive our lives with
the symbols of faith and speak the stories of our lives with the
language of faith can this experience become revelatory and
exemplary to others. The power of such narratives should not
be in doubt. No one who has attended the meetings of Alco-
holics Anonymous misses how the narrative of personal experience can not only relate but also effect conversion. Such
narratives can also of course be abused, and used manipula-
tively, as when "testifying" in a church replaces sober and difficult personal discussion and discernment. Narrative is
therefore an ambiguous and untidy theological medium. But
insofar as it is in touch with experience and insofar as it becomes the means through which experience can reach public
expression in the church, it remains an essential means of
discerning God's work in the world. When Paul has to choose
between the demands of intellectual consistency and the demands of the experience of God in human lives, he always
allows experience to take precedence. It is an instinct the
church has not always, not even now, followed.

The Choice for Conscience.   Given the overall perception of
the Pastorals as concerned with order and reflecting the rou-

tinization of charisma, it may be a bit shocking to find Paul
defending the primacy of faith, conscience, and the heart as
determinants of moral behavior rather than the interpretation of laws. But such in fact is the case. And Paul makes this
defense not against the claims of a code alone but against
those whose "morbid craving for controversy and for disputes
about words" (6:4) would erect around the law an impene-
trable thicket of behavioral norms, intelligible (and therefore
interpretable) only by experts, the "teachers of law." This re-
liance on conscience is closely connected to Paul's insistence
on experience as the basis for shaping our lives. It is, after all,
only our internal mechanisms of moral consciousness which
enable us to "discern" in ambiguous experience the work of
God. Just as religious traditions prefer to rely on precedent
rather than on lived experience, indeed, want whenever possible to fit the experience of God within neat precedents, so
also the same instinct places a premium on code rather than
conscience. To rely on the judgment of individual conscience
is too unpredictable. To base decision making in the church
on the reciprocal process of experience and discernment is
too terrifying. The quite understandable human tendency is
to seek to control experience (and therefore God) within the
framework of law and its interpretation. Understandable as
well is the human desire to flee the awful demands of forming
and exercising a responsible adult conscience. How tempting
and how much more secure to turn ourselves over to the
moral experts who can codify our lives. Yes, says Paul, but
such is not the way of the "dispensation of God." God's way of
working in the world, exemplified by the conversion of Paul,
is through the ambiguity and complexity of human experience. We cannot abdicate our conscience, for if we do, we
shipwreck the whole response of faith.

Behavior at Worship (2:1–15)

Timothy was not only to silence opponents but also to deal
with community problems, including those concerning reading, preaching, teaching (4:13). When Paul takes up the question of behavior at worship, he pens one of the NT passages
most offensive to contemporary sensitivities. The passage as
a whole tends to be overshadowed by the problems posed by

its last section. Yet it is reading the passage as a whole which gives us help in understanding the historical setting of the discussion as well as the possibility of a responsible pastoral appropriation of it.

Paul is far from providing the Ephesian church with a "church order." Although his general topic here is worship, for example, he gives no instructions concerning its time, place, or contents. Those are all presupposed. Paul treats only two topics: the saying of prayers for others (2:1–7) and behavioral norms for men and women (2:8–15).

Paul's instruction on prayer is short but leads us into a symbolic world shared by him and his readers, although in many ways strange to us. Paul takes it for granted that "supplications, prayers, intercessions, and thanksgivings" (2:1) should be a part of worship. He tells the Philippians also, "by prayer and supplication with thanksgiving make your requests known to God" (Phil 4:6). But here he indicates the range of their prayers in two ways, the first conventional, the second less so. We are not surprised that he wants them to pray "for kings and all who are in high positions" (2:2), for in the empire, the king was regarded as head of the whole "household" of the civilized world (*oikoumene*). Among the "household duties" of all people, therefore, was respect and obedience to the emperor.

The social order is of all things most conservative and resistant to change. Social arrangements work effectively in fact only to the extent that they are regarded as "natural" or "inevitable" and not the arbitrary creation of human will. Only the radical pluralism of the modern world, together with its unprecedented awareness of the multiple possibilities for human societies, have led to a "sociology of knowledge," which enables us to perceive social structures as the constructs of human intentionality. Visions of alternative societies were not totally unknown in the ancient world: Plato's *Republic* was thoroughly utopian and reformist. But under the empire—which was by the time of Paul the only real political fact in the world for over three hundred years, much longer than the whole history of the United States—such alternatives were not seriously entertained. The most massive fact available was this: a single hierarchical order reached from the top to the bottom of the "human family," an order in which authority moved downward and submission moved upward. Moralists had further solidified this symbolic world by taking it as given, and asking "what are the duties (*ta kathekonta*) of the various members of society within this structure?"

It is difficult for us who live in fragile if not fragmented social worlds to appreciate the sheer facticity of that ancient order. It was generally regarded, in fact, as part of the *oikonomia theou*—the dispensation of God. Nature and society were part of the same continuum, all of which was governed by God's will, or "providence." To deviate from the norms of the social order, then, was really to deviate from "nature" and from God's ordering of the world. The point of these observations is simple: it was as impossible for Paul to have envisaged a Jeffersonian Democracy as it was for him to have imagined the contemporary nuclear family with dual-career spouses. His instructions were for a world not only different from ours structurally, but even in conception. Part of the "symbolic world" we live in, after all, is the concept that society *is* in fact a changeable thing. Precisely that perception would not have been Paul's as a human being of the first century. There may have been good or bad emperors but surely there would always be emperors!

It is crucial for us to understand these connections, for they enable us to better appreciate much of what Paul says in this chapter. We understand thereby why kings and rulers should be prayed for. A religious community thus expresses its proper place in the order of things. We also can see here (as in Rom 13:1–7 and 1 Peter 2:13–17) how inevitably affirmative of the given social order earliest Pauline Christianity was. At the time these letters were written such fundamental propositions as these—that the Emperor's authority came from God (Rom 13:1), or that rulers "are not a terror to good conduct, but to bad" (Rom 13:3), or that governors were sent by emperors to "punish those who do wrong and to praise those who do right" (1 Peter 2:14)—did not require questioning. Only the hard experience of persecution at the hands of an emperor precisely for being a Christian shook these automatic equations and enabled Christians to see for the first time that the state also could become demonic (see Rev 17:1–18).

Paul's motivation for such prayers is not surprising, either: "that we may lead a quiet and peaceable life, godly and respectful in every way" (2:2). He expressed this same sentiments in other letters (1 Thess 4:11–12; 2 Thess 3:12; Col 4:5–6; 1 Cor 14:23). A quiet and orderly life not only nurtured the work of the Spirit (see 1 Cor 14:33), it also earned the respect of outsiders. The Christian community, deviant enough in others ways, did not need to draw attention to itself, particularly since the empire was suspicious in principle of groups that met regularly in convocation.

What is surprising in Paul's opening instruction is his desire for the community to pray "for all [people]" (2:1). This is the element "above all" (2:1) that Paul wants to stress and which he supports theologically (2:3). Before discussing the meaning of the instruction, however, it is necessary to note how an (unconsciously) androcentric translation makes the interpretation difficult for those without access to the Greek original. Notice that in 2:1, the RSV translates "for all men." Likewise in 2:4, "God . . . desires *all men* to be saved" (author's italics), and finally, Jesus the mediator is the "one man" (2:5). The problem with these translations is that they are inaccurate and misleading. In each case the Greek term is *anthropos*, not *aner*. It is not *males* for whom the community is to pray, but all people; God wills the salvation of "all people;" it is not the *maleness* of Jesus which makes him mediator, but his humanity. These translations would be problematic in themselves. But in a passage where Paul proceeds to make distinctions between male and female, they become intolerable. Without the Greek, for example, one could oppose 2:4 and 2:15. God wills the salvation of all *males* and that they reach the knowledge of truth. But *women* can be saved only conditionally through bearing children and cannot reach the knowledge of truth (see 2 Tim 3:7). Clearly, this is not what Paul means. But the English translation would allow such a reading.

Yet, it is Paul's extension of prayer to "all humanity" which is most striking here. The earliest Christian writings generally confined themselves to intra-community relations, ex-

pressed succinctly as "love of the brethren" (1 Thess 4:9).
Outreach was limited: "So then, as we have opportunity, let
us do good to all [people], and especially to those who are of
the household of the faith" (Gal 6:10). But here we find the
logical extension of Paul's vision in Rom 9–11, expressed both
as a theological principle and as a community practice based
on that principle. They are to pray for all people, and this is
pleasing to God because "[God] desires all [people] to be
saved and to come to the knowledge of the truth" (2:4). It is
for this principle that Paul has been made "a preacher and
apostle . . . teacher of the Gentiles in faith and truth" (2:7).
His mission, in turn, is based on the *oikonomia theou*, the way
God has revealed his will in the world (see Eph 3:1–14). Paul
bases the universal salvific will of God first in God's own sin-
gularity: "God is one." We remember this as the axiom (found
first in Israel's *Shema*; see Deut 6:4) on which Paul also based
the principle of righteousness by faith (Rom 3:29–30). If God
is to be more than a tribal deity, then he must be God of all
humans. And if God is to be "righteous" then he cannot rig
the game; all must have equal access to him. Access cannot
be restricted to those who have a special revelation or secret
code, even if it is a genetic code!

Paul adds to the first principle a more paradoxical statement: "there is one mediator between God and humans, the
single human being Messiah Jesus" (2:5). At first, this appears
to be opposed to the first statement for it reintroduces the
element of particularity. But Jesus is the single mediator not
on the basis of his teachings, deeds, or even as an object of
belief but on the basis of his very humanity: Jesus is the representative human before the one God. His mediation is
found first in the humanity he shares with all of us. Second,
"[he] gave himself as a ransom for all" (2:6). Jesus' life and
sacrificial death were for all human beings. Certainly, an element of particularity remains. Paul sees "the knowledge of
the truth," after all, as the recognition of Jesus as this mediator. But the element of the universal extension of salvation is
even more noteworthy. However Jesus functions as mediator,
God truly "wills" that all people reach salvation. Nowhere in
the NT is there such an inclusive expression of hope. It is particularly important to note its presence here, for it stands as

the functional equivalent of Gal 3:28: "There is neither Jew nor Greek, there is neither slave nor free, there is neither male nor female, for you are all one in Christ Jesus."

Paul next turns to the instructions concerning men and women. About the men, he has little to say. He presupposes their dominant role in worship according to the precedent set by the Diaspora synagogue. There is increasing archaeological evidence suggesting that women played a more active role in the governance of synagogues than we had suspected, but certainly for the most part men played the chief liturgical roles in public, with women's role restricted to the domestic Sabbath celebration. Paul wants the men in every place to lift up their hands in prayer "without anger and quarreling" (2:8). Such divisive attitudes are inappropriate to the fellowship of the Spirit at any time (see Phil 2:14) but particularly so in periods of communal prayer. Do we detect here, however, a somewhat sharper edge to Paul's remark, dictated by the situation Timothy faces?

We recall that the "house of prayer" (*proseuche*) also functioned as a "house of study" (*beth hammidrash*) for the interpretation of Torah. The two activities were not rigidly separated; each was a glorification of God. Reading and prayer flowed one into the other. Discussions of texts (midrash) alternated with periods of silent private and vocal public prayer in a daylong preoccupation with God's word. If this Ephesian church borrowed such procedures from the Diaspora synagogue—and the model was certainly ready to hand (see Acts 19:8–10)—how natural it would be for some discussions of texts to overflow into the prayer. And if these discussions were characterized by "anger and quarreling," such attitudes could in turn disrupt the prayers. In fact, we know that there were people in this community who wanted to be "teachers of the Law" and who devoted themselves to speculation and disputations over words. Perhaps Paul's rebuke reminds all those who would allow disputation over Scripture to become distorted, of what really joined them together: prayer before the one God.

Paul's first instruction concerning women is joined to that concerning the men by the connective, "likewise" or "in the same way," indicating the rough equivalence of the directives

(2:9–10). Women should be adorned with "good works" not with elaborate hairdressing, jewelry, or clothing. Such is "fitting" women who profess to be religious. The word "fitting" is significant here. It reminds us that Paul is dealing precisely with the cultural perceptions of his age. In this whole discussion, we are in the realm of the customary, and therefore, by definition, in the realm of the conservative.

When Paul decries elaborate clothing and makeup for women, he is at one with his fellow Greco-Roman moralists. This was overwhelmingly a patriarchal society. With some notable exceptions, property, inheritance, and public authority were invested in men not women. In such a society, women going alone into public places, women speaking in public, or women dressing with great elaborateness were automatically suspected of acting like prostitutes. It is that simple. If an intentional community such as the Christians wished to avoid the slanders directed against groups like the Epicureans (that they were dens of iniquity because they gave equal access to women) then it would need to look at what was and was not considered "fitting" for women. There is an even more elaborate version of this same *topos* in 1 Peter 3:1–6. We can recognize the same level of concern as well in Paul's discussion of the veiling of women when they pray or prophesy, in 1 Cor 11:3–16. There, he throws up a flurry of cultural presuppositions with great heat but little light about women's "head" and "hair" and how they are either honored or dishonored. In that passage, Paul finally has to recognize that his rule about veils is not really based in any theological axiom. Indeed, he systematically refutes himself (1 Cor 11:11). The rule is based on the *custom* of all the churches, which is after all not an unworthy reason: "we recognize no other practice, nor do the churches of God" (1 Cor 11:16). But if we are in the realm of custom, then however much Paul and his fellows equated "custom" and "nature," if we see that they cannot be so equated, then the custom can change. At the same time, one might ask whether Paul's distinction here between outward (and/or seductive) adornment and inward virtue is not one that can be applauded and used within quite different circumstances or social structures.

It is the second of Paul's instructions for women that most

offends contemporary readers: he commands women to be +
silent in the assembly (2:11–15). The central issue here is her-
meneutical not exegetical, so I will discuss the text with as
much dispatch as possible, leaving some room for a consideration of the pastoral problem. The basic problem is that we ⌐
not only have a command to deal with but also a theological
rationalization of it.

In contrast to Paul's discussion in 1 Cor 11:3–16, the context for this command is not prayer and prophecy in the as- ⌐
sembly. Paul apparently had no problem with women doing
those things, nor could he have, since they were the work of
the Spirit, and "the spirits of prophets are subject to prophets" (1 Cor 14:32). The context here is rather like that sug- ⌐
gested by 1 Cor 14:33b–36: the setting of teaching and
learning. In the synagogue as in Hellenistic culture generally, ⌐
however much women were initiated into the ecstatic mani-
festation of religion, even functioning as prophetesses and
oracles, the interpretation of sacred texts and the teaching of ⌐
morality were regarded as masculine responsibilities. Phar-⌐
isaism was militant in this regard, and Paul was very much
a Pharisee in his perceptions concerning Torah. Whatever
role women played in their children's education (and Paul
could give that considerable credit, see 2 Tim 1:5), it was domestic and private. The perception that moral instruction
was a male prerogative was ancient in this patriarchal world
(see Prov 2:1; 3:1; etc.) even though Wisdom itself was often
personified as feminine (see Prov. 1:20–33; 8:1–31). The paradox may be only apparent. As recent scholarship has indi-⌐
cated, the patriarchal structure of Roman culture was
sporadically challenged by the wealthy women of leisure who
joined cults or philosophical schools. We have already seen ⌐
the problems concerning sexual reputation that attached to
some of them. And, for the most part, the patriarchal perceptions held sway. Certainly they did in Judaism, and above all
in the Pharisaic tradition, which so much shaped Paul's perceptions of what was "fitting."

Paul's command, "I do not allow" is consistent with his
statements in 1 Cor 11:16 and 14:33b–36, although here he ⌐
does not support it with "the practice of all the churches" (1
Cor 14:33b, author's translation). His command that women

keep silence (twice in 2:11–12) and learn in all submission
substantially agrees with 1 Cor 14:35, "If there is anything
they wish to know, let them ask their husbands at home, for
it is shameful for a woman to speak in church." The note of
submission is, however, even sharpened in this passage: "I
permit no women to teach or to have authority over men"
(2:12).

Paul's theological warrant for his command forms a chiasm
to the instructions. The women is not to have authority because she was created after man and is therefore by the order
of creation subordinate to him (2:13). She is not to teach because teachers should not be easily deceived (see 2 Tim 3:13)
and women, like Eve, can be deceived and fall into transgres-
sion (2:14). Paul uses the argument from the order of creation
also in 1 Cor 11:3, 8, and the "deception of Eve" story from
Gen 3:1–7 also in 2 Cor. 11:3, although there he applies it to
the Corinthians' tendency to be taken in by charlatans. Paul
generally finds the Adamic myth instructive (see Rom 5:12; 1
Cor 15:45–49), though ordinarily by way of *contrast* to this
new age. The support for his injunction here is his reading of
a narrative in Torah. It is striking that in 1 Cor 14:34 he states
"they should be subordinate as even the Law says," whereas
here he makes no such direct appeal. Is it because the "Teachers of the Law" would be only too eager to engage that issue?

Paul concludes his discussion with a concessive clause:
"But she will be saved through bearing children if they remain in faith, love, and holiness, with modesty." The clause
creates more confusion than clarity. Some possibilities can be
eliminated. The suggestion that Paul here speaks of the birth
of the Messiah through "the woman" Mary has no merit. It is
also unlikely that he simply reverses the Genesis curse—that
women would be subordinate to men and experience childbirth in pain (Gen 3:16)—by saying that she will be "brought
safely through childbirth," for the subject of "if they remain"
must—contrary to the RSV—be plural, referring to the woman's children, not herself. This much might be said about the
concluding phrase. Paul does not make women's "salvation"
in the proper sense depend on their having children. That is
sufficiently clear not only from 2:4 above, but from the rest of
Paul's letters. Neither does Paul see "childbearing" as a

purely biological function. He connects the children's "re-maining" in these virtues with the woman's role, however ob-scurely. The best resolution of the exegetical difficulties, I think, is to take the final statement as a concessive corollary of the refusal to women of a public teaching role or rule over their husbands. They do have a role in educating their chil-dren in virtue. It is obviously a narrower role but a real one nevertheless, and some would even argue that it is more im-portant than the other.

*   *   *   *   *

I am strongly tempted to reflect on Paul's statement, "God wills the salvation of all humans," for it is the very heart of this passage and stands as one of the noblest expressions in the NT, normative not only for ecumenism but also for the internal life of the church, foreclosing at once sectarianism as well as elitism of the gnostic or Marcionite variety. Alas, such a discussion would be pastorally remiss since the final section of this chapter most demands attention.

I presuppose here the general statements made in the intro-duction to this letter concerning the difficulties posed by commands and their warrants and move directly to this text. Its reception in the church today is challenged for two rea-sons. First, it conflicts with our hard-won convictions con-cerning the fundamental equality of women with men and the necessity for truly reciprocal relations between them. Second, it conflicts with passages in Paul which support that deeper level of egalitarianism: "There is neither . . . male nor female . . . in Christ Jesus" (Gal 3:28).

Some would seek to solve the problem by denying the pas-sage Pauline authorship. The "real" Paul is egalitarian; only the "Pastoral" Paul is patriarchal. The solution won't work for two reasons. First, this statement is completely consistent with Paul's basic approach in 1 Corinthians. Attempts to make 1 Cor 14:33b–36 an interpolation fail for lack of evi-dence and literary logic. No, in this matter, even if 1 Timothy is pseudonymous, it agrees with the "real" Paul. The tension between subordination and equality is found in the "real" Paul, too, as even the most casual glance at the book of Phi-lemon will confirm. Second, the text does not derive its authority (and its potential to scandalize) from Pauline authorship or lack of it but from its status as part of the canon of Scripture, which is read in the assembly and used as the normative framework for ecclesial debates over identity. It is as "God's Word" and not as "Paul's word" that the text is edifying, scandalizing, or both at once.

2. A second solution works by way of censorship. We reject the authority of this text for us. It may be canonical but we do not regard it as "God's Word." Why? Because Scripture and God's word are not coextensive. As a general theological proposition, this is inarguable. But as a specific textual solution it is inadequate. If this text is not authoritative for us because it does not agree with our convictions concerning women's identity and we will not have it read to us, what then shall we do with all the other texts with which we do not agree? Do we, like Marcion, eliminate the whole OT—he because it was sponsored by the evil demiurge responsible for matter, we because it sponsors patriarchalism?

Do we not listen to Jesus's words on divorce and oaths because we in fact divorce and swear in courts of law? Do we stop reading Rom 1:18–32 because we think homosexuals also have civil rights and are not necessarily depraved and corrupt? Do we not read Philemon because we do not believe slavery is right? And if so, do we also refuse to read Phil 2:5–11, because it portrays Jesus as a slave and presents his life of submission as a model for all Christian existence? Such is the direction of the censorship option. Texts are authoritative only insofar as they appear to agree with our own perceptions. In effect, we recognize as Scripture what is ideologically compatible with us. We can look at these texts and see ourselves as in a mirror. If this practice becomes general enough and exercised vigorously enough by all interested parties, we would lose the text altogether, and with it, the edge of difference between ourselves and the primordial and normative expressions of our identity. We will hear, grow used to hearing, rationalize hearing, only what we like to hear. It is critical to note, however, that the "authority" of a text does not mean that it necessarily supports our action or justifies our existence in a one-to-one fashion. A text is an "authority" or "normative" most of all because *it must be taken into account*. We do not discuss or debate our identity—or rules—in the church without using all the canonical texts as the basic and indispensable boundaries to the discussion.

A better solution, then, is the one I have been edging to- *3* ward throughout this discussion of 1 Timothy. It is a more complex and messier solution, but it respects both the au- ‿ thoritative nature of the text and our continuing experience of God in the world. If we thus enter into a living and critical dialogue with the text (exercising criticism both on the text and on ourselves), we come to several important recognitions.

We recognize first that the critical problem lies not so much in Paul's words themselves as in the history of their reception ‿ and interpretation. The answer to that, however, is certainly not to abandon the text but rather to change the direction of its application! The text demanding the silence of women in ✝ the assembly is by itself no more binding as a rule for today's church than the command not to wear jewelry or to pray for the emperor. The commands are time-conditioned and relative and very much affected by the social upheaval created by Paul's opposition, who were, in fact, "deceiving" women in the assembly.

Our experience and growth in awareness (a growth abetted by passages such as Paul's "neither male nor female") no ‿ longer allow the perception of women as subordinate to men by nature or divine will nor the perception that they are "weaker" or more easily "deceived" than men. Whatever Genesis says, such perceptions are no more valid than the one that it took seven calendar days to create the world. Nothing ‿ in Paul's text or its canonical status prevents us having women teaching in church, being ministers, or holding positions of authority over men, any more than Paul's directions on idol meat dictate our dining habits today. Nor is there anything in his use of the Genesis story which could be construed as a fundamental hostility toward women. This text itself ‿ stands in tension with 2:4 "God wills the salvation of all humans and that they come to the recognition of the truth" (author's translation).

Because Paul's time-conditioned and occasional words were made a part of Scripture, however, they were absolutized by the history of interpretation. And in an age increasingly hostile to women (I am thinking of the patristic writers of the second through fifth centuries), the text did become an instrument of terror and suppression in the hands of its interpreters, justifying things Paul would never—could never, I submit—imagine or countenance. If his words about silence and submission in the assembly are taken out of their narrow liturgical/pedagogical context and made the excuse for discrimination or wife beating or psychological tyranny, then they indeed have become enslaving.

But what if we stop reading and interpreting these texts publicly in the assembly, and interpreting them in the light of our Spirit-led growth in knowledge? Then, we will not change anything! We will leave the text for private and ignorant interpretation, which has always proved disastrous. We need above all to confront (be confronted by) and interpret these hard texts in the public assembly, precisely so that we can gain by interpretation freedom from those parts of them that could bind us and be bound in turn by those parts of them that can free us. We need continual reminding of how we stand at a distance from them and why we stand at a distance from them. We need to consider over and over again the *grounds* of that distance. Otherwise, in a cruel paradox, we allow the very limited patriarchalism or androcentrism of Paul to become at the popular and practical level a destructive and virulent sexism.

But if we allow these texts to speak to us in the assembly and if we can hear in them the tension between an egalitarian ideal and the resistance of social structures to the realization of that ideal, then we are reminded that such tensions will always exist. Neither do we perfectly realize the reconciliations Paul saw as the norm in Christ. We too deal always with resistant social structures which demand boundaries, role definitions, and authority structures. So long as we are human we will struggle with these as well as with sexual prejudices of every kind. The most important lesson we can learn from texts like these is how to recognize the dimensions of the issues within which we too must continue to live.

Qualifications for Leadership (3:1–16)

Paul's differentiation of roles for men and women at worship in 2:8–15 leads rather naturally to the discussion of overseers (bishops) and deacons in 3:1–16. The emphasis here, however, is not on what they are to do but on what sort of personal qualities they are to demonstrate. Paul provides no job description for bishop or deacon; we are just able to grasp that one rank might lead to another (3:13). So little does Paul provide an organizational chart that we can still argue today about the sort of structure this community had.

More immediately pertinent to Paul is filling the positions with qualified people. It is too seldom recognized by readers of 1 Timothy that this community seems to have had a genuine crisis in leadership. Timothy was not, after all, put there as a trouble-shooter for no reason. When we look closely at the letter, we can see that the threat posed by the would-be teachers of law is made worse by the inadequacy of the current community leadership. There are signs of deficiency in intellectual, managerial, and even moral qualities. Notice, for example, that Paul needs to discuss charges brought against elders in 5:19, and mentions those who "sin before all" in 5:20 (author's translation). He warns Timothy not to appoint people to leadership roles precipitously—suggesting thereby that mistakes had been made along these lines (5:21). Consider that Paul has to sort through the whole issue of the care of widows, because there is presently confusion—an administrative confusion—concerning who should be served in this way and who not (5:1–16). Observe that wealthy members of the community need to be warned not to grow "haughty" or presume on their riches; perhaps they were in fact moving into leadership roles without appointment (6:17). Notice how Paul has had to intervene personally to excommunicate Hymenaeus and Alexander (1:20), which, as in the case of 1 Cor 5—6, points to a lack of will to exercise strong judgment within the community.

These pieces of evidence suggest that Paul's listing of qualifications for leadership in the community did not arise in a vacuum but was generated by a real historical context of failure. The concentration on certain kinds of "virtues" or capacities is also not purely formal but directed to a perceived need.

When we review the qualities desired in the overseer, for example, we are impressed by the emphasis put on moral stability and managerial prowess. To be a bishop, says Paul, is a desirable thing—although the RSV's "office of bishop" greatly overformalizes the Greek. The one who is a candidate for this role, however, must first of all be "above reproach." We see at once that the overseer is to play a public and representational role in the community. Thus, a recent convert (neophyte) should not be appointed lest conceit overtake him and he "fall into the trap of the devil" (3:6, author's translation). For the same reason, the overseer must enjoy a good reputation among outsiders (3:7). The Greek is a bit ambiguous in both statements, making us uncertain whether the overseer who grows conceited or the overseer who has a bad reputation comes under the influence of Satan (see 2 Tim 2:26), or falls prey to slander. In either case, the concern is obviously with how outsiders are going to perceive the community.

The virtues sought in the overseer are not those of the charismatic. To be the husband of one wife, temperate, sensible, dignified, sober, and without greed (3:2–3) is not to be a figure of great romance. But it is to have the character required for the long haul of institutional stability. Certain specific features emerge. We notice that the overseer is to be an "apt teacher," reminding us of Timothy's charge to appoint others who could teach (2 Tim 2:2), and preparing us for the discussion of those who "labor in preaching and teaching" in 5:17. Throughout these letters, the dominant image for the ministry of the word is "teaching." We observe here as well that the *manner* of this teaching is to follow that prescribed in 2 Tim 2:24: the bishop is not to be violent or quarrelsome, but "gentle" (3:3).

Finally, we see the overseer is to be "hospitable" (3:2), which points us to the social realities involved with this role. To be hospitable requires that one have a household; to be a householder means to have at least a certain measure of wealth. Not only was hospitality a remarkably important virtue for the earliest Christians—since their mission required travel and their holiness forbade staying in inns which were largely brothels—but those who could provide the assembly with a place large enough to meet and provide provisions for traveling missionaries, quite naturally also assumed roles of leadership (see, for example, 3 John; Heb 13:2; Philem 1–2; Rom 15:24; 16:1–3). The connection is stated implicitly by Paul in 1 Cor 16:15–18: "Brethren, you know that the household of Stephanas were the first converts in Achaia, and they have devoted themselves to the service of the saints; I urge you *to be subject to such men* and to every fellow worker and laborer. I rejoice at the coming of Stephanas and Fortunatus and Achaicus, because they have made up for your absence; for they refreshed my spirit as well as yours. *Give recognition to such men*" (author's italics).

In 1 Tim 3:4–5 the ability to manage one's own household is regarded as a criterion for caring for God's church (3:5), which is itself also "the household of God" (3:15): "He must manage his own household well, keeping his children submissive and respectful in every way" (3:4). We remember the perception of the social order: authority runs downward, submission upward. If the head of a household (*paterfamilias*) has rebellious children, he will certainly not be able to handle the refractory "teachers of the law" either. Although the church is imaged as a "household of God," however, it does not follow that its structure is precisely that of the private household. As we shall see, it appears as far more collegial than the ordinary household. In 1 Timothy the church as intentional community remains distinct from the households of its members (see also 5:4, 16). The ability to manage a private household serves as a criterion precisely because the two institutions remain separate, yet the skills demanded in one are transferable to the other.

The qualifications of deacons are similar to those of overseers. Again, moral probity ranks over prophetic gifts: seriousness, sobriety, lack of greed (3:8); marital fidelity and management skills (3:12). We note the caution characteristic of these lists. Candidates are to be put through a period of probation before they serve as deacons (3:10); "for those who serve well ... gain a good standing for themselves" (3:13).

They must also "hold the mystery of the faith with a clear conscience" (3:9; see 1:5). But what do deacons do? We are not given the slightest clue; all that is presupposed.

Equally puzzling is the exact significance of 3:11: "The women likewise must be serious, no slanderers, but temperate, faithful in all things." The passage is obscure on several counts. Does it refer to the wives of the male deacons? Or does it refer to female deacons? That women held such positions from the start is proven by the case of Phoebe, "deacon of the church at Cenchrae" and Paul's patron, whom he sent to Rome to prepare his expedition to Spain (Rom 16:1–3). And we know from the later church orders that women also functioned as deacons at least in certain liturgical capacities. On the other hand, the notice is very skimpy, and in the light of 2:11–15, surprising. Nevertheless, there can be no real doubt that it refers to women deacons. First, the statement is introduced by "likewise" (hosautos) as in the case of the male deacons (3:8); separate consideration is given to this group as also to bishops and male deacons. Second, if it referred to wives of male deacons it would be out of sequence, since attention to them would better follow, "They should have one wife" (3:12, author's translation). Third, on the other hand, mention of "the women" could well have reminded Paul of that further qualification for male deacons. Fourth, in addition to the women's moral qualities, they are required to be "faithful in all things," which suggests the carrying out of community responsibilities (see, for example, 1 Cor 4:2). It should not be necessary to belabor the rather obvious point that this diaconal function stands in contrast to the interdiction of women's teaching in 2:11–15. I suggest that this once more indicates the narrow and specifically pedagogical focus of that earlier passage.

We will have an opportunity to describe more fully the overall structure of this community when we discuss chapter five. For the moment, however, it is appropriate to note how relatively simple and lacking in sacral trappings these functions appear to be. Not only are the relative responsibilities of overseers and deacons not meticulously catalogued, there seems to be no concern that they should be. The offices, furthermore, are entirely practical, organizational, matter-of-fact. There is not the slightest hint of "priestly" language, for example, or even of "servanthood." Indeed, we find *no* theological legitimation for these positions. This is the more striking if we place 1 Timothy against another document deriving from a first-century Jewish sect, the *Community Rule* of Qumran. There we find not only a community with an elaborate hierarchical structure but also with the most intense form of rationalization of that structure in terms of the community's overarching symbols. Likewise, if we look in the other direction we find in the Letters of Ignatius of Antioch (ca. 115 CE) a similarly elaborate presentation: bishops stand as monarchs over their churches, with priests and deacons arrayed around them. Each position, furthermore, has its own theological rationalization. I imply no value judgment, but simply register the observation that we are dealing with something much simpler and more straightforward here in 1 Timothy. That is why I find the RSV's translation, "office of bishop" problematic, since it seems to imply the presence of only one such figure in the community. Simply in terms of what the text reveals, we would picture the situation as closer to that suggested by Phil 1:1, where Paul greets "all the saints in Christ Jesus who are at Philippi, with the overseers and deacons."

Paul closes this section (or perhaps opens the next section, since the literary transitions here are not obvious) with a flourish typical of this letter, which characteristically juxtaposes the banal and the sublime. Paul notes that all these directions have temporary application until his return (3:14). Then he shifts into much more formal language, concerning "how one ought to behave in the household of God, which is the church of the living God, the pillar and bulwark of the truth" (3:15). This is already a fascinating concatenation of images: the commonplace one of the household, operative till now, shifts to "the assembly of the living God" which is not only more classically Pauline (see Gal 1:13; 1 Cor 1:2), but also considerably more dynamic. This "household" is one where one meets, after all, "the living God" (see 1 Thess 1:9). Then in an even more violent transition, Paul overleaps the assembly and returns to an architectural image. The church is called "pillar and bulwark of the truth." Yes, but what does this mean? The terms translated "pillar" (see Gal 2:9) and "bulwark" mean practically the same thing in Greek: in some sense, the community "supports" the truth. Together the terms suggest solidity and strength. They do not, however, suggest that the church and the truth are coequal or that the church is the only place the truth can be found. These are tendrils of triumphalism which have grown up around Paul's more modest architectural image. The point of his statement, I think, is that the community is more than an organization or even a "natural grouping," like a household or family. It is a convocation called together by the living God, and it lives by something more than its structure or its human affections: it derives its life from that "truth" which is the experience of the living God.

If this is correct, we can perceive as less violent the subsequent transition to the great "mystery of our religion" in 3:16. The language of mystery is congenial to Paul (see Rom 11:25; 16:25; Eph 5:32), often being used for God's revealing the reconciliation of Jews and Greeks in the church. The statement of the mystery here bears the marks usually associated with traditional or even hymnic material predating Paul: the opening relative pronoun, the rhythmic strophes, the parallelism, and use of the passive voice. This fragment fits the pattern of "mystery once hidden but now revealed" found elsewhere in the NT (see Rom 16:25; Col 1:26; 1 Peter 1:20).

The point of the recitation here is not instructional. Paul does not need to give Timothy a doctrinal lesson. Rather Paul shares with him, in the midst of this recital of ministerial qualifications, a small but powerful reminder of what all the structure is for: to reveal the mystery of God's presence in the world.

* * * * *

What could be less fascinating than these dry lists of qualifications? What could offer us less inspiration? Yet perhaps that is part of their value and potential for preaching. The church of God over the centuries has often been distorted by an overemphasis on structure to the neglect of prophecy so that the church came to appear a factory for salvation. But the church also has at times been so seduced by the attractions of charism that its structures have been neglected. And when neglected, structures tend to become self-perpetuating and all devouring. It is somewhat sobering to observe just how simple and straightforward 1 Timothy is on these issues. Just that stringency should stand as a judgment on communities—however elaborate or simple their "official" structure—whose life is in the process of being swallowed by procedures, meetings, and paperflow.

In a similar fashion, the virtues of these first-century administrators do not appear as overly heroic. Indeed, they are sometimes dismissed by commentators as a form of "bourgeois" piety, a sign of the church's "accomodation to the world." Actually, this dismissal is overhasty on several counts. First, the judgment that structure is incompatible with eschatological fervor or charisma, so that talk about structure is a sign of declining spirit or expectation of the end, should by now be no longer credible. Not only the clear documentary evidence of Qumran from the past, but the present experience of sectarian movements of all stripes reminds us that most often structure and charism can coexist, often indeed coexist in mutually rigid and reinforcing ways. Second, the virtues of sobriety and marital fidelity may seem trivial to those with a romantic outlook on reality. But the majority of human beings for whom escape into drink or drugs is often more than a little attractive, and for whom a sexual adventure with someone other than one's spouse is often extremely desirable, find that these virtues represent a sort of quiet heroism, won day by day. When exemplified by persons who must be visible to the world and to the community on a continuing and public basis, such virtue is even more remarkable. Finally, these down-to-earth organizational capacities should not be ignored when communities make decisions concerning their leaders. Sometimes a community has suffered from a lack of effective preaching or prophecy and thinks that it wants as an overseer or pastor a person of charismatic gifts. Or it seeks both charisma and efficiency. Most often, the gifts do not come together, and reflecting over lists like these in 1 Timothy can provide a helpful starting point for the debate and discussion required of the assembly that must make such a decision.

The Good Minister of Jesus Christ (4:1–16)

Following the pattern of alternation characteristic of this letter, Paul turns from instructions concerning worship and qualifications for leadership (2:1—3:16) to the personal exhortation of his delegate Timothy. This chapter therefore strongly resembles 2 Timothy, above all in the way Timothy's attitudes are contrasted to those of the opponents.

The appearance and activity of the opponents is here attributed to the eschatological conflict of the last days (4:1). The apocalyptic conviction that the end-time would be marked by apostasy, deceit, and false prophecy was widespread among the first Christians; the battle for the truth was not carried out simply at the ethical level; it involved as well a cosmic struggle between spiritual forces for good and for evil (see, for example, 1 John 2:18; 4:1; 2 Peter 2:1; Mark 13:22–23; Matt 7:15; 24:23–24; Eph 6:10–15; 2 Cor 10:1–6; 11:12–15; 2 Thess 2:9–12; Rev 13:11–18). Paul does not therefore need to cite a specific text when he asserts, "the Spirit expressly says" (4:1); the scenario was universally recognized.

In 2 Timothy Paul warns also of the stress caused by "the last days" when hostile actions and treacherous attitudes would characterize people (3:1–5; 4:3). In that letter too the opponents were regarded as "caught in the snare of the devil" (2:26, author's translation). The apocalyptic outlook is even more intense here: some are "abandoning the faith" and are "involving themselves in deceitful spirits and demonic teachings" (4:1, author's translation). Paul adds two phrases which are characteristic of these opponents in 1 Timothy: they speak with "the hypocrisy of liars" (or "through the pretensions of liars") and "their consciences are seared" (4:2). For all their deceit, they lean more toward rigor than laxity. Paul uses another medical term when he says their consciences are "cauterized." He means at least that their moral awareness is desensitized. In the light of this description, we can better appreciate his insistence in 1:5 on a "pure heart, good conscience, and unhypocritical faith," since these people are abandoning the faith, are hypocritical, and have seared consciences.

Paul commands Timothy to avoid their "godless and silly

myths" (4:7) which is typical of polemic, but he also indicates the results of their lucubrations over "the law." They "forbid marriage and enjoin abstinence from foods" (4:3). Furthermore, they appear to advocate a "physical training" or asceticism (*somatike gymnasia*, 4:8). From our usual perceptions of the Pharisaic tradition after the destruction of the Temple in 70 CE, it is difficult to see how the study of Torah would lead to an ascetic life. The forbidding of certain foods may follow from the laws of purity, but how could marriage be banned in the rabbinic tradition?

In fact before the triumph of Pharisaism, the sedulous study of Torah could lead to just such conclusions. We know that even sages within Pharisaism who practiced merkabah mysticism observed at least temporary sexual and dietary continence, as a preparation for their flights of prayer. The sectarians at Qumran and the Therapeutae in Egypt were also Jews who tended toward sexual and dietary asceticism, while being very much attached to the interpretation of Torah. The Christian movement also shows us how matters of diet and sex were much disputed. If some in Corinth went to prostitutes and ate at idol shrines, others wanted strict observance in diet and declared, "it is well for a man not to touch a woman" (1 Cor 7:1; see chaps. 8—10). Paul also had to rebuke some in Colossae who combined observance of Law with physical asceticism and mysticism as essential marks of "maturity" (see Col 2:8–23). Typical of such teachers of the law is that they "forbid" (1 Tim 4:3)—they impose on the behavior of others their own perceptions of what the law demands. As Thomas Merton once sagely observed, "the ascetic starts off being hard on himself but ends up being hard on everyone else but himself."

Before looking at Paul's response, we need to consider the logic involved in applying the law this way. The prohibitions, "do not touch a woman," "do not eat (this food)," derive from a perception of the world in which certain things and activities are either so powerful that they are dangerous or are so "unclean" by nature that they also "pollute" the one using them. Certain foods are forbidden because they are "unclean" and render unclean the eater. But why would marriage be forbidden? The line of illogic seems to run from the perception that women are "unclean" at certain times (because of menstrual cycles and childbirth) to the perception that women are generally "unclean" and therefore polluting of men by the act of intercourse. This perception, in turn, can be joined to a radical dualism and reach even higher levels, to the point that any "contamination" of the spirit by matter is dangerous, since matter itself (the changeable, fickle realm of the body) is fundamentally incompatible with the realm of the "spirit" (where being, beauty, and truth alone can be found). Although in the command, "it is good not to touch a woman" the misogyny may be logically only secondary, it is nevertheless misogyny of a real and powerful sort. It is also far more ontologically rooted, and therefore immovable, than Paul's "let a woman keep silent."

In his exhortation to Timothy to "be a good minister (*diakonos*) of Christ Jesus" (4:6), Paul employs some of the motivations he also uses in 2 Timothy. He reminds Timothy of the gift he has received from God. He is "not [to] neglect the gift in you which was given through prophecy and the imposition of hands by the board of elders" (4:14, author's translation). We notice here the taken-for-granted harmony between the work of the Spirit (prophecy) and the human appointment (by the hands of elders). The same combination is found in the selection of Paul and Barnabas as missionaries at Antioch (Acts 13:1–4). Acts does not relate any such ordination for Timothy, although in 2 Tim 1:6, Paul says that Timothy was appointed "through my hands." What Paul wants to emphasize in this reminder is that in the "gift" given to Timothy the prophetic Spirit of God is at work. Opposed to this are only the "deceitful spirits" of the charlatans. For Paul, it is an unequal battle.

As Paul in 2 Tim 3:10 reminds Timothy of the teaching and way of life he had "followed" in observing Paul, so here he proposes that Timothy be "nourished on the words of the faith and of the good doctrine which you have followed" (4:6). If he lives according to the pattern of these, then he can himself be a model for the community to imitate (4:12). He is not only to teach them properly ("in speech"), but also is to illustrate the proper understanding in the way he lives ("in conduct," using the same term—*anastrophe*—as in 3:15, "How one ought to behave in the household of God"), which Paul spells out in shorthand: "in love, in faith, in purity." Timothy is to let nothing deflect him from this role. He is not to waver if some should "despise [his] youth" (4:12). Yet, as a young man, he cannot pretend to present to the people a portrait of finished virtue. Paul therefore tells him, "[Let] all . . . see your *progress*" (4:15, author's italics). The term "progress" (*prokope*) is just one of the educational terms Paul uses in this section. It often refers specifically to progress in the moral life. Even as a young man, therefore, Timothy can model the struggle for virtue and demonstrate how one can grow in the qualities of faith, love, and purity.

Paul also provides Timothy with the proper understanding (the "good teaching") by which he can refute the opponents and instruct the faithful. He does not explicitly take up the issue of forbidding marriage, simply because he does not need to with this delegate. Timothy surely shares his perception that marriage is not only a legitimate gift from God (1 Cor 7:7) perfectly compatible with holiness (1 Thess 4:3–4), which can sanctify both spouses and children (1 Cor 7:14) and even stand as a symbol of the reconciling work of God in the world (Eph 5:32), but that it is also declared indissoluble by the Lord himself (1 Cor 7:10). Neither Paul nor his delegate would regard celibacy as a requirement for Christians, however desirable they saw it for themselves (see 1 Cor 7:7; 2). Paul can also assume that what he has to say about the role of food in the created order covers the topic of marriage, since the reasons for "prohibiting" or "allowing" one apply as well to the other.

In Paul's response, we recognize the characteristic "strong" position which he adopts in his First Letter to the Corinthians (chaps. 8—10). No part of the world is in itself evil or contaminating. The use of our bodies in sex and in matters of diet must therefore be regulated by "conscience," that is, by the careful balancing of freedom with responsibility to God, ourselves, and others. Here, however, we find an even more universal and positive statement than in 1 Corinthians: "everything created by God is good, and nothing is to be rejected if it is received with thanksgiving" (4:4). No part of the world lies outside God's will or power. What was stated in Gen 1:31 still holds, "God saw everything that he had made, and behold, it was very good."

But does then Paul pull back from this by twice affirming, "if it is received with thanksgiving" (4:3–4)? Does "thanksgiving" change the nature of things, so that something otherwise unacceptable becomes acceptable by the magical efficacy of prayer? To think so would be to misunderstand what Paul means by "thanksgiving" (*eucharistia*). Like his fellow Jews, Paul saw the prayer of thanksgiving as an *anamnesis*, a recollection of the presence and claim of God in the world. More than a formal recitation of words, it "blessed" God and "glorified" God by recognizing—often using the very words of Torah—how all things came from God and also returned to him: "there is one God, the Father, from whom are all things and for whom we exist" (1 Cor 8:6). This sort of recognition does not "change" God's creation physically, but it does transfigure the world by the powers of human intentionality and freedom. Humans gladly acknowledge that they and all things come, every moment, from God. And with that recognition, they help establish in fact the world as "God's creation" in which all things are clean. Without such acknowledgment in thanksgiving, the world is of course no less God's! But as the realm of human freedom, it becomes distorted. When the world is not referred to its maker, it grows grotesque and misshapen: "although they knew God they did not honor him as God or give thanks to him, but they became futile in their thinking and their senseless minds were darkened" (Rom 1:21). But when food—or sexual love—is celebrated with such humble recognition and gratitude, Paul regards it as "consecrated" in double fashion: by the word of God which created it, and by the prayer of thanksgiving which rejoices in it as God's work (4:5).

Paul has no more patience with the pretensions of physical asceticism (4:8), whose style of forbidding this and that he castigates in another place: "these have indeed an appearance of wisdom in promoting rigor of devotion and self-abasement and severity to the body, but they are of no value in checking the indulgence of the flesh" (Col 2:23). The term "flesh" here has little to do with physical excess but much to do with spiritual arrogance. These ascetics in Colossae had the tendency to judge, condemn, and disqualify those who did not meet their standards of maturity (Col 2:16, 18). They thus revealed themselves to be, in the Pauline sense, "fleshly," that is, hostile and unloving (see 1 Cor 3:3; Gal 5:19–21).

Instead, Paul wants Timothy to "train yourself in godliness" (4:7). However elliptically, Paul makes thereby a very important distinction between two kinds of spirituality. One sort of spirituality identifies "the spirit" with the human psyche and seeks to realize its full potential by the control of the body and mental processes. By Paul's measure it is a spirituality which can grow self-centered, closed to both God and neighbor. Paul calls it of "little usefulness," for it mainly functions as a way of "perfecting" ourselves, so that we can measure our accomplishments over against others. In contrast to such spiritual narcissism, Paul places "training in godliness." The "Spirit" here is not an aspect of human potential but is the gift of God. Such a spirituality sees the "struggle and labor" of human existence not as a process of increasing control over physical and mental habits but as a continuing openness to the call of God and the needs of the neighbor. Such "training in godliness," Paul says, is "useful in every way." It is not compulsively closed in on the self but is capable of every action and attitude demanded by faith in its response to the call of God, moment by moment. The two modes of spirituality are contrasted also in this: the spirituality based in physical asceticism is useful only for this life. That which is centered on God looks for a share in God's own life not only now but in the "life to come" (4:8). Its "promise" is not limited to the closed horizon of human potential but is open to the infinite horizons of God's life. Notice how Paul secures this by the sure saying (4:9): "For to this end we toil and strive, because we have set our hopes on the living God, who is the savior of all [people], especially of those who believe" (4:10). The contrast is absolute between the self-striving of human potential, and the gift of life from "the living God."

With such a deeper understanding of the shared tradition

does Paul want Timothy to instruct the community: "Take
heed to yourself and to your teaching; hold to that, for by so
doing you will save both yourself and your hearers" (4:16).

* * * * *

Paul's instructions to Timothy on marriage, diet, and physical asceticism had a critical role historically in defining the
limits of authentic Christian spirituality, particularly against
the flood of radical asceticism which over-ran the Mediterra-
nean world in the second century and which, in the guise of
Gnosticism and Marcionism, nearly submerged Christianity
itself. His statements on the goodness of the created order
stood as a "bulwark of the truth" against elitist movements
which demanded celibacy and fasting of everyone as a corollary of baptism. Still more, they protected the truth of the
incarnation against the "Paulinists" who attributed the phe-
nomenal world to an evil demiurge, claiming that the only
way to salvation was through the denial of the body. His clear
statement that God was the Savior of all persons stood
against all those claiming that only the "gnostics" or "illu-
minati" or "spiritual" could be saved, and that all others
(even in the church) would simply return to the evil matter
from which they came. It was undoubtedly because of such
statements that Marcion could find no place in his truncated
Pauline canon for the Pastorals. By doing violence to the intention of Paul's other letters, Marcion could derive an ascetical brand of Christianity. But not even violence could make
1 Timothy yield anything other than its "good teaching": the
gospel of God encompasses and sanctifies all of creation.

No great distance separates the ascetics of the second century and some contemporary spiritualities. The perspectives
of Paul are of more than purely historical pertinence.

How much difference is there, after all, between those who
would "forbid marriage" in order to achieve a freedom from
the created material order, and those who would, for the sake
of "realized human potential" consider marriage as an entrapment or at best a compromise entered into with reluc-
tance or dismay? Is there really a massive distance between
those who said "do not eat" because of a fear of impurity
caused by cosmic iniquity and those who today say "do not

eat" because of a fear of contamination caused by cosmic conspiracies? Is there much difference between the ancient ascetic devoted to physical self-control for the freedom of his spirit and the contemporary physical fitness freak who compulsively punishes his body so that he will "reduce stress" and live longer?

The bond between the asceticism of old and that of today, however different they appear on the surface, is the perception that human perfection is realizable in this life only. The horizon of human hope is set therefore by our accomplishment.

If our human worth is established only by a "successful" professional career and salary, then yes, marriage with its endless consumption of our energy and time and enthusiasm in the care for spouse and children is a trap (for both man and woman) which closes us off from our potential or "essential identity." If carcinogenic foods rob us of precious moments from our life, then they are indeed demonic, once we agree that these moments are all we will ever have. And if my physical health or longevity is my only expectation for life, then I do well to protect compulsively myself from all danger, preserve my vital fluids, and expend every effort to extend my few precious moments.

What Paul has to say to these perceptions is still scandalous. He says they are made of myths and foolishness. Our striving is to share God's life in the future even as now every moment we live comes from him. God is our perfector. We should rejoice in the entanglements of the body and spirit, for they are the result of God's creation and train us in true godliness, so that we can "in that day" share the genuine and eternal life that comes only from "the living God, who is the Savior of all" (4:10).

The Care of Widows (5:1–16)

Paul again turns to the concrete community problems with which Timothy is expected to deal. His first exhortation (5:1–2) is so general that it seems almost without content; but it leads to a second concern (5:3–16) which is so specific and complex that its untangling is a notorious problem for the history of earliest Christianity.

Paul advises Timothy first on the attitudes he should have toward persons of various ages and genders within the church. He is to treat older men as though they were fathers, younger men as brothers, older women as mothers, and younger women as sisters—with all purity (5:1–2). General as it is, this short exhortation does yield some important information. First, the advice coheres with this letter's overall picture of Timothy as a young man (see 4:12). Second, it reiterates the Pauline insistence on gentleness rather than harshness; Timothy is not to be "abusive" to older men but is to exhort them as if they were his own father. Third, the advice shows us how factors of age and gender impinge even on an "egalitarian" community of "brothers and sisters." Real-life persons are no more simply "brothers and sisters" than in a totalitarian state they are "citizens X." Age and gender require specific and appropriate attitudes. The advice here touches on the typical temptations of a young male delegate: to be overweening in the exercise of authority over older men; to be seductive in the care of younger women. Finally, the language Paul uses shows us again how fluid was the terminology regarding rank and office. Scholars sometimes wonder whether in 5:1 Paul is telling Timothy not to rebuke an "elder" of the church. Surely not, but the ambiguity in language reveals how far Paul is from establishing a sacralized church order. And because this is a stage when "natural" kinship relations and "institutional" ones can overlap, we meet the major problem with which Paul must now deal: the care of widows in the community.

I have suggested several times in this commentary that the structures of the church found in 1 Timothy most resemble what little we know about the structure of the Diaspora Jewish community of the first centuries CE, a structure loosely identified by the term "synagogue." I have also suggested that this structure was readily available to the Pauline communities. In this chapter, the point of such observations will become clearer. To help make them so, a few more words of historical filling may be useful.

The little we know of synagogal leadership indicates that it had a group of "elders" (the *gerousia*) who had responsibilities for the community's finances and for the handling of internal community disputes. There were also one or more "rulers of the synagogue" (*archisynagogoi*), who sometimes appear as founders, patrons, administrators, or all three at once. Their relationship to the "board of elders" seems to have been about the same as that between the "overseer" and the "board of elders" in 1 Timothy. Our main problem with the sources from both traditions is that they tell us so little of what we would like to know. Just such matters of internal organization are taken for granted. Who today in a college bulletin takes the time to explain the typical structure of a seminar as opposed to a lecture class? Who needs reminding in our culture of how committees proceed? So also here. In any case, we also know of a lower level synagogal functionary, called the *chazzan*, who carried out liturgical and perhaps other functions. The *chazzan* seems roughly equivalent to the *deacon* in 1 Timothy.

The synagogue (also "house of prayer" and "house of assembly") provided the Jewish community a place for its social realization. It was a house of worship (reading of Torah, preaching, prayers) and a school for the study of Torah (teaching). It was a place for settling community conflicts. It was also—and this brings us to the point—the place where the community's almsgiving was carried out.

Each local Jewish community took on the responsibility of caring for its own dispossessed and poverty-stricken members as well as the provisioning of visitors. There were two basic forms of dispersal. The first (called "the dish") was much like a soup kitchen, providing food and other immediate needs to wayfarers or those temporarily impoverished. The second (called "the chest") provided longer-term assistance to those of the community whose income or support was gone. In this category would be the women and children who had lost their husbands and fathers. Since biblical times, "orphans and widows" were the classic victims of an economic system which was land-based and patriarchal. When their providers died, they were left without any aid except that which could be given by the community.

Taking seriously the biblical injunctions to "do justice" and care "for the poor of the land," Jewish communities adapted ancient techniques of support (reserving a corner of the field, storing grain in the city) into these more flexible mechanisms of aid. It was a burdensome responsibility. The rabbinic sources are filled with the praise of almsgiving (called "acts of righteousness" as in Matt 6:1 where the RSV reads "piety"), but also with complaints about the difficulties of its practice. Careful consideration is given to the moral rectitude required of the collectors of charity and money, and above all, of those who disperse such funds. The community appointed two men for each role. They could thus more easily decide difficult cases and could also keep an eye on each other to protect the community's money from fraud. It was arduous to collect money from those who were themselves often painfully poor. But how much harder to be fair in the distribution of limited funds! In these sources, we find the perennial problems of all relief systems: who qualifies? how do we determine the greatest need? what are the limits of care? how do we determine fraud?

We know from Acts 6:1–3 that the first Jerusalem community of Christians continued this practice in its daily feeding of the widows. We also learn from the passage that the question of who gets cared for, who counts as a ward of the community, was raised in a highly disputatious fashion. We meet the same issues in this passage.

The transition is provided by the instruction, "treat ... younger women like sisters, in all purity" (5:2) which leads naturally to "Honor widows who are real widows" (5:3). It is an odd phrasing, but the issue seems to be, "who should qualify for community care under the category of 'widow'?" This is indicated by the way the discussion is framed. Paul's main concern is for the respective responsibilities of private families and the community as a whole. Three times in the section (5:4, 8, 16), he makes it clear that the community should not have to bear an unfair burden and that those who are able to provide financial support for their own family members should do so. Once again, we find that the structure of the private household and that of the community is separate, however much each may in some respects resemble the other.

Paul insists that children and grandchildren owe a "religious duty" to their parents, adding, "this is acceptable in the sight of God" (5:4). That children must "honor" their parents is of course one of the Ten Commandments: "Honor your father and your mother, that your days may be long in the land which the LORD your God gives you" (Exod 20:12). That Paul took this command seriously is indicated by Eph 6:1: "Children, obey your parents in the Lord, for this is right," quoting Exod 20:12 in support of his exhortation. That such "honor" included financial support of parents is shown by the anger of Jesus at those who would put aside this responsibility by the clever reading of Torah (see Mark 7:9–13). For children in a household not to support their parents but put them on the community dole is therefore to neglect a serious religious duty. Paul heightens this even further in 5:8 when he says, "If anyone does not provide for his own people—and especially members of his own household—he has denied the faith and is worse than an unbeliever." This is extraordinarily strong language. Certainly such a one has denied "faith" in the sense that he has failed in loyalty and filial piety. But Paul pushes further than that. Such a person is worse than an unbeliever, because even pagans cared for the members of their household, even if they did not have communities of sharing such as those maintained by Jews and Christians. Like the incestuous man of Corinth (1 Cor 5:1–5), the uncaring children of Ephesus fall below the minimal standards of community integrity by their neglect of their parents.

The practical motive is mentioned in 5:16. Private care should be exercised whenever possible so that the community resources will not be overtaxed and so that the church can take care of those who are "real widows." This last exhortation is fascinating above all because Paul has in view the responsibility of a "faithful woman" toward her widowed parent. We learn thereby that some women are wealthy or "rule their households" (5:14) and so could take on such financial responsibilities. What emerges from these remarks, then, is that households should whenever possible provide for their own members' financial care and that the church as such should take on the responsibility only for those who are "true widows."

This leads us to the next question: what constitutes a "real widow" and why should such a distinction be necessary? Paul did not have to qualify himself, for example, by speaking of "real" younger women in 5:2. Although the subsequent discussion appears complicated, it is actually rather straightforward. The essential condition is genuine financial need. She has been left all alone. The woman has no family or friends who are in a position to provide her with regular support for the rest of her days. The burden on them would be too much. And she has no other expectations. The second stipulation is that she is really a member of the "household of God." This is indicated by her life of piety: "She has set her hope on God and continues in supplications and prayers night and day" (5:5). A "real widow" is therefore not only someone whose husband has died but a woman left alone in the world, in financial distress, who is at the same time a faithful member of the community. Paul contrasts her situation with that of the "false widow"—"she who is self-indulgent is dead even while she lives" (5:6). Self-indulgence is available only to those who have some means. Some women who are technical widows, therefore, (whose husbands have died), have the means to support themselves, and have less than a real commitment to the life of faith. The financial support of such people is not the community's concern.

But then, how can one in specific cases determine the "genuineness" of the widow's faith? Paul proceeds in 5:9–10 to take up that most ticklish of tasks. These qualifications, it should be noted, do not touch on the issue of need. A widow should be "put on the list," Paul says, only if she had already shown herself to be a certain caliber of person. Some scholars take this term "put on the list" as an "enrollment" in a special "order of widows," and then proceed to draw historical conclusions therefrom. This impression is further suggested by the RSV's translation in 5:11 "do not enrol," which is simply mistaken. In that place, Paul simply says, "avoid younger widows," and in this place, he simply indicates who should be put on the list of charity recipients. I see no evidence for a formal "order of widows" in this letter.

The qualifications are threefold: age, moral probity, and service to the community. The reason for the age limit is rather clear. An elderly widow does not have the problems discussed by Paul in 5:11–13. Also, the community can com-

mit its limited resources to her more readily, since she will
need it fewer years than someone very young. The woman's
moral character is shown by her fidelity to one husband, her
good deeds, and her rearing of children. Her service to the
community has been manifested by her actions when she herself ruled a household: she has "shown hospitality, washed
the feet of the saints, relieved the afflicted, and devoted herself to doing good in every way" (5:10). For such women, the
financial support of the community is truly an honor shown
those who have already "parented" the community as a whole
and, therefore, truly deserve life-long support in fulfillment
of a "religious obligation" (see 5:4).

The reasons why Paul's elaborate list of qualifications is so
necessary appear in 5:11–15. The community is experiencing
some problems with younger widows. Their husbands have
died, it is true, but their youth and sexual desires and lack of
proven virtue makes their continual and official support by
the community problematic. We encounter again the concern
for the community's reputation with outsiders on these delicate matters of sexual customs. We must remember that an
intentional community of "brothers and sisters" outside the
conventional boundaries of the household was already cause
enough for suspicion in the eyes of some. Pagan critics of
Christianity were quick to exploit polemically the lubricious
suggestions of "incest" found in "brothers and sisters" ex-
changing the "kiss of peace." Paul wants to "give the enemy
no occasion to revile us" (5:14) or the women themselves to
"incur condemnation" (5:12). But in fact, this is already happening, for "some have already strayed after Satan" (5:15).
What is happening here?

To appreciate the potential for offense, we must imagine
the situation: a group of young women are being financially
supported by a group of "elderly men" who are in no way
related to them! What distinguishes them in the eyes of outsiders from "kept women"? If the women on the dole are elderly and are of excellent reputation for virtue, there is less
possibility of offense. But if they are youthful and sexually
eager (however we translate the difficult "growing wanton
against Christ") and seeking a mate ("desiring to marry");
then the possibility of scandal grows.

Paul obviously has no problem with the younger women wanting to marry—this is exactly what he wants for them as well: "I would have the younger widows marry, bear children, rule their households" (5:14). But a young woman with that goal in mind and the community should not pledge themselves to each other. When a widow is supported by the church, she is pledged to its service "and continues in supplications and prayers." But if widows are being supported without being willing to devote all their energies to the church's needs—and why should they when they are young and healthy—when they want to marry, they are regarded as having broken their pledge, and are condemned. This is unfortunate enough. But Paul also indicates that some young widows are in fact acting very irresponsibly. Taking advantage of the community's financial support and their own freedom from household responsibilities, they have become gadabouts and gossips, "saying what they should not" (5:13). In effect, the integrity of the church is in jeopardy if it sponsors a group of young, sexually interested and mobile women, who make a habit of going "from house to house" (5:13). The community should not bear the financial or moral responsibility for what appears to be something of a dating service, if not worse. Paul's advice to Timothy is concise: avoid younger widows.

* * * * *

This discussion reminds us again how difficult it is to move from specific directives in the past to rules for the church today. Social structures (public and private) and perceptions of sexual roles are very different now than they were in Paul's time. Impossible now for a community to institute and maintain the sort of regulations Paul proposes. Yet this passage remains of vital importance to the church's life in every age.

First, it reminds us that sexual decency is a problematic and delicate issue for all intentional communities. So long as humans are both male and female, neither the denial of sexual differences and attractions nor the exploitation of them will have any consequences other than disastrous. We may find Paul's perception of the widow's virtue archaic, even quaint. Yet, what harm has come to communities whose professed standards of sexual behavior have first been cynically betrayed and then degraded! Healthy sexual relations between those who are "one in the Lord," yet not committed to each other in marriage, cannot simply be taken for granted. If Paul's understanding of "purity" is not our own, what have we in place of it?

Second, the difficulty of determining who is a "real widow" in our own communities remains painfully alive. "Doing justice" is not an easy and self-evident thing when one gets down to hard cases. The questions arise of whom the community should commit itself to in financial support and on what grounds of reciprocity; what belongs to the responsibility of private families and what to that of the whole community; how can fraud be avoided without inquisitorial techniques, trust maintained without exploitation; what are the limits of care, once we go past the daily bread and soup? These are achingly familiar questions. We do Paul a disservice by not recognizing them as being fully as real then as now. We do ourselves a disservice by refusing to face them now with as few illusions as Paul did then.

Third, and most significantly, the passage reminds us forcefully of the fundamental and unavoidable *obligation* to support those without the means to support themselves or without others to help them. The issue for Paul was what fell to individual families and what fell to the church as such. It would have been inconceivable to him to push it all off on the state. The doing of justice is not a mechanism for economic leveling; it is the direct and appropriate care of the needy among us, according to their need. What would Paul have thought of us who lobby for social legislation but do not see the (literal) widows who devote themselves to supplication night and day in our own communities? What would Paul have said to those of us who betray the most elementary demand of nature, not to mention of the Ten Commandments, by leaving the care of our parents to anonymous institutions, because we simply cannot be bothered?

Problems with Elders (5:17–25)

Paul turns next to a series of directives concerning the elders, who in all likelihood formed a leadership council (*presbyterion*, 4:14) responsible for financial and judicial administration in the church, analogous to the *gerousia* of the Diaspora synagogue. Although the other Pauline letters do not mention the office of elder, Acts shows us Paul appointing such elders in churches (Acts 14:23; see Titus 1:5) as well as delivering his farewell discourse to these "elders of the church" at Ephesus (Acts 20:17). Other NT writings indicate that the arrangement was widespread (see Acts 11:30; 15:4; James 5:14; 1 Peter 5:1; 2 John 1; 3 John 1).

The relationship between this board of elders and the other leaders discussed in this letter (bishops and deacons) is not altogether clear. In the present passage, we observe that the fundamental activity of the elders is called "ruling" (*prohistemi*, 5:17), which would probably include administrative and judicial duties. Paul elsewhere uses this term when discussing positions of leadership. Although the RSV translates Rom 12:8 as "let ... [him] who gives aid, [do so] with zeal," the Greek reads, "let him who rules do so with zeal." Likewise in 1 Thess 5:12, Paul says, "Respect those who labor among you and are over you (*prohistemi*) in the Lord and admonish you." As for exercising judicial functions in the community, Paul chides the Corinthians because they take disputes to Gentile courts, asking them, "If then you have such cases, why do you lay them before those who are least esteemed by the church ... Can it be that there is no man among you wise enough to decide between members of the brotherhood, but brother goes to law against brother, and that before unbelievers?" (1 Cor 6:4–6). Clearly, Paul would have them settle such cases before the "esteemed" members of the community, which in Corinth would likely have been those "first fruits" and men of substance such as Stephanas (see 1 Cor 16:15–18).

The ability to rule is also one of the qualities looked for in both overseers (3:4) and deacons (3:12). Furthermore, we observe that some of these elders "labor in preaching and teaching" (5:17), while we have also seen that the overseer is to be an "apt teacher" (3:2). If, finally, we note that in Titus 1:5–7 the membrane separating overseer and elder is an exceedingly permeable one, we can reach this broad but generally satisfying picture of the Ephesian administrative structure: while it was the responsibility of the whole board of elders to handle the finances and exercise judgment for the community, these functions would be coordinated by one of their number (temporarily or not, we cannot tell) called the overseer. In all likelihood, this overseer would be chosen not only because of his age (or tenure in the community) but because of his special administrative gifts. Some of the elders including the overseer would also teach. The deacons were lower level administrators, probably carrying out the practical needs of the liturgy and charity distributions. If something like this structure is assumed, Paul's directions here make good sense.

Paul takes up first the question of payment. Those who exercise the ministry of the word in addition to administration should receive "double honor." There is little doubt that "honor" here bears its financial sense; we have already examined the financial implications of "honor thy father and mother." Although there was some debate on the matter among philosophers, the general rule was that the spiritual benefits of wisdom should be repaid with material benefits (see Gal 6:6; Rom 15:27). Paul's own practice of preaching to the Corinthians without pay was an exception (1 Cor 9:18; 2 Cor 11:7), made possible, in fact, by the support he received from the Philippian community (2 Cor 11:9; Phil 4:10–14). It was a practice, moreover, which lent itself to charges of deceit and fraud (see 2 Cor 12:14–18). When Paul discusses his own practice, furthermore, he insists that he also has the right (*exousia*) to such payments, as do the other apostles (1 Cor 9:6–14). In support of that position, he quotes the precedent established (by midrash to be sure) in Deut 25:4, "You shall not muzzle an ox when it is treading out the grain" (1 Cor 9:9). Paul quotes the same passage here (1 Tim 5:18) in support of the payment for elders. Likewise in 1 Cor 9:14 Paul supported the pay of ministers by reference to the command of Jesus, "In the same way, the Lord commanded that those who proclaim the gospel should get their living by the gospel." Here, Paul cites that saying of Jesus directly (as found also in Luke 10:7), "The laborer deserves his wages" (1 Tim 5:18).

Second, Paul must deal with charges brought against elders by members of the community. I suggested earlier that the emphasis on qualifications for leaders in this letter may owe something to failures among the present board of elders. Paul invokes immediately another principle from Torah (Deut 19:15): "A single witness shall not prevail against a man for any crime or for any wrong in connection with any offense that he has committed; only on the evidence of two witnesses, or of three witnesses, shall a charge be sustained." This essential principle of fair judgment is an obvious protection against arbitrary charges brought by the disgruntled or those carrying out personal vendettas. It is established also as a rule for the church in Matt 18:16 and is strikingly invoked again by Paul in 2 Cor 13:1. That Paul here has to tell Timothy "never admit a charge against an elder" except on this basis surely indicates that such charges are being made.

That there were reasons for the charges is also made clear from Paul's next two directives. Those who persist in sin (the RSV rightly gives a strong reading to the present participle of "sinning": they continue to sin even after being exposed by a charge) are to be rebuked by Timothy before all the rest of the elders, so that they "may stand in fear" (5:20). They are, in short, not to be protected or excused. They are to be made an example. Furthermore, Timothy is not to be hasty in the laying on of hands (5:22). By allowing wrongdoing to fester in the leadership ranks or by appointing unworthy people to those positions (through carelessness or haste), Timothy in effect will "participate in the sins of others," and Paul wants him to "keep himself pure" (5:22).

As a delegate of Paul's who must at once correct abuses and refute opponents, while also strengthening the local leadership, Timothy is in a difficult, indeed almost impossible, position. The gravity of his mission is emphasized by Paul's charging him to follow these directives "in the presence of God and of the elect angels." And Paul holds him to a very high standard. He is to do everything "without prejudice or partiality" (5:21). That a judge should be no respecter of persons was axiomatic in Israel (Lev 19:15). For Paul such "impartiality" describes the utter righteousness of God as judge (Rom 2:11; 3:22; Col 3:25; Eph 6:9). Here, he makes it the standard that Timothy is to observe!

Paul's final instructions in 5:23–25 are difficult to construe.

While they make some sense individually (though not a great deal), they are even more problematic when read in the present context. Why does Paul tell Timothy to stop drinking only water? Perhaps it is because Paul's previous instruction could have been misconstrued, with Timothy thinking "keep yourself pure" (5:22) meant such abstinence in diet? Or perhaps Timothy himself was attracted to the sort of physical rigor advocated by the opponents (see 4:8–10), a rigor Paul himself found so deceptive? In any case, it is clear that for Paul, "purity" is not defined in terms of physical or ritual observance, but in terms of ethical attitudes and behavior (see 4:12; 5:2, 22). What, then, are we to make of his last remarks? They are harder to understand in the Greek than in the English (the RSV has done well with the intrinsic obscurity). The main point seems to be that the real character of people will be shown by their behavior over the long run, however they might appear on the surface. Although some sins are public and cry out for reaction, others are hidden and only slowly appear. The same for good behavior; good deeds, even if not "conspicuous" will eventually come to light. Yes, but why say that here? Is it to remind Timothy that he should be patient in his role as judge, waiting for all the evidence to appear and not be a "respecter of persons," that is, deceived by external appearances? Or is it personally directed, so that Timothy should not be overimpressed by the "surface piety" represented by physical asceticism, either in others or in himself, for one's deeper character will always come to light in the end? Both readings are possible; neither is certain.

* * * * *

Once more, the challenge this passage presents to the church in our age comes not from the specific directives themselves, so much as the contemporary nature of the issues dealt with here for every church and the utter realism with which Paul confronts them. Three short propositions can perhaps stimulate a process of reflection and lead to sermon construction.

If a church is to be a *church* and not a sect, it must have ways of dealing with failure and even sin. A sect, defining itself in terms of a realized perfection, has no other choice in the face of failure than to divide itself again. But a church must find ways to reveal and heal moral sickness within it. It must do this even, or especially, when it is the leadership of the community which is diseased.

If a church is to live according to the standards of "impartiality" mandated by Scripture (and the Lord), then it must have *just procedures* for the resolution of these failures and sins. In the case of leaders, Paul offers some helpful guidelines: the church cannot dismiss its leaders on the basis of idiosyncratic complaints or whispering campaigns. Charges must be openly stated and supported, "by two or three witnesses." On the other hand, those who do wrong when in positions of leadership cannot be protected and camouflaged, for to do so is to corrupt the church itself. Just as the charge against them should be open, so should be their penalty: "They should be rebuked before all, so that the rest might take fear."

If a church is to continue to be a *community of holiness* and maintain its distinctive identity in the world, it must learn itself how to exercise judgment within. As Paul insists in 1 Corinthians, the community has the responsibility for maintaining its own standards. When wrongdoing or corruption in the community are not dealt with "by the saints," then at some point they will be dealt with by referral to outside authorities. When that happens, there is no more community, only a loose assemblage of litigants.

Wealth and Social Status (6:1–23)

The final section of 1 Timothy combines all the distinctive elements of this letter: (a) careful attention to practical problems of the community, this time the role of the rich (6:17–19) and the attitude of slaves (6:1–2); (b) polemic against the false teachers with a specific rebuttal of their position (6:3–10); (c) the positive portrayal of Timothy the teacher (6:2b, 11–12); and (d) the final solemn commandment of Paul to his delegate (6:13–16, 20–21). The elements remain somewhat disjointed literarily, so no great violence is done them if they are considered topically rather than in the order of their textual appearance.

The popular image of earliest Christianity as a proletarian

movement attracting only the impoverished and enslaved still persists, although it is much oversimplified. In fact, there were wealthy members from the earliest period of the movement, at least in the urban Pauline communities. Paul tells the Corinthians that there were not many powerful or well-born among them (1 Cor 1:26), but the statement itself suggests there were some, and we meet them in the figures of Stephanas, Fortunatus, and Achaicus, who provided the churches hospitality as well as financial support for "the saints" (1 Cor 16:15–18). Paul's fellow workers Aquila and Priscilla undoubtedly enjoyed sufficient wealth to enable their frequent travels (see Rom 16:3; 2 Tim 4:19; Acts 18:1, 18, 26) as well as to provide hospitality for the church that met in their household (1 Cor 16:19). Phoebe the Deacon of Cenchrae was wealthy enough to be one of Paul's patrons (Rom 16:1–2).

The presence of wealthy members in the congregation necessarily created tensions at several levels. On the one hand, the rich were expected to contribute generously to the needs of the church. On the other hand, they could receive for their generosity no special treatment or authority. More than anything else, this denial of their social role as benefactors made their life an uncomfortable one. In the Hellenistic world, the wealthy were expected to practice liberality and share their possessions with those less well off. But when they did so, they were regarded as benefactors and were seen to have a special claim over those they helped, even if this relationship was not formalized by the patron-client bond. But in the church, the image of ministry as servanthood—undoubtedly introduced by Jesus himself—turned those social arrangements upside down: "The kings of the Gentiles exercise lordship over them, and those in authority are called benefactors. But not so with you; rather let the greatest among you become as the youngest, and the leader as one who serves" (Luke 22:25–27). If this were not deflating enough, the rich were also sometimes brought under suspicion or even condemnation for being wealthy in the first place (see Luke 16:9, 13; James 1:9–11; 5:1–6).

Typical of his approach elsewhere, Paul does not here condemn the rich but only warns them of the peculiar dangers to which their wealth exposes them: the assumption that wealth gives them power and the notion that wealth gives them true security. The first danger he counters with the command, "not to be haughty" (6:17). Just because they are "rich in this world" does not mean that they have any advantage with God or that they have any particular authority in the community, even if they do contribute to its welfare. Second, he does not want them to place their hope on "uncertain riches," for they provide no true security. Rather, they are to "lay a good foundation for the future" by placing their hope in God. Paul uses here the language of the Gospel; they can "lay up treasure for themselves" of a more lasting sort (see Matt 6:20). They are able to do this because they do not equate their identity and worth with their possessions but with what is "given richly for their enjoyment" by God (6:17, author's translation). This is the gift of "real life" (or "life itself," 6:19). Because they are established in their identity by the gift of God's life and because they hope in him, they are free to share their possessions with others liberally, without any need for recompense, even the honor of being called "benefactor." So Paul piles up the phrases denoting such sharing of wealth: they are to "do good, be rich in good deeds, be liberal in giving, share possessions!" (6:18, author's translation).

The social order of the Roman Empire received another shock with the conversion of slaves to the Christian movement. Just as when women listened to men not their own husbands it was considered a threat to the stability of the household, no less was it shaken by the "liberation" of slaves who, by sharing in the same baptism with free people, became "brothers and sisters in Christ" with them. It was clear to no one in the beginning how the egalitarian ideal of "in Christ there is neither slave nor free" could be combined with the demands of the social order, "slaves be obedient to your masters." The tension was there from the beginning, nowhere more graphically illustrated than in Paul's Letter to Philemon. However much he wants Philemon to receive back the runaway slave Onesimus "as a beloved brother" and not simply as property (Philem 16), however much he wants Onesimus liberated from the service of Philemon to "serve" in the mission (Philem 13, 20), the fact remains that Paul sent the slave back to his owner, recognizing Philemon's legal rights (Philem 18).

Paul's basic approach to this issue, as to others involving human distinctions, was to deny their *fundamental* importance for human identity and worth. Before God all humans are equal, however much they may not be so in law or custom. For Paul, furthermore, it is our standing before God which is the only status which ultimately matters, for it is the only truly ultimate thing. He consistently refuses to identify any human condition as being either an aid or a hindrance for our standing before God. It does not help to become a Jew if one is a Gentile, "for circumcision means nothing and uncircumcision means nothing, but a new creation" (Gal 6:15, author's translation). It does not help to eat certain foods or to change marital status (1 Cor 7:21; 8:8). The same applies to the condition of human servitude: "Were you a slave when called? Never mind. But if you can gain your freedom, avail yourself of the opportunity. For he who was called in the Lord as a slave is a freedman of the Lord. Likewise he who was free when called is a slave of Christ" (1 Cor 7:21–22).

Paul's advice to Christian slaves here is consistent with his approach elsewhere. They are to pay their masters all honor "so that the name of God and the teaching may not be defamed" (6:1). The concern for the community's reputation and therefore for its safety emerges here again. But Paul adds a special word of advice for those Christian slaves whose masters also happen to be Christians (which was the case also with Philemon and Onesimus). Paul recognizes the tendency of such slaves to "despise" their masters. This could be for two reasons. Either the masters failed to carry out the egalitarian ideal of "neither slave nor free" by actually freeing their slaves or they did not carry over into the daily life of the household the attitudes of "brother and sister" found in the liturgy but demanded obedience to their orders. Paul perceives that this "inconsistency" could easily be seized on as a basis for "despising" their masters. Paul's advice is rather dramatic, and its full force can only be appreciated in the Greek. He says first that masters who are Christians should receive even greater service *because* they are members of the community

rather than because of a legal obligation: they are, after all,
"faithful and beloved." This is remarkable enough, but Paul
continues with a stunning paradox. He calls the masters
"those who receive your beneficence" (*euergesia*, 6:2, author's
translation). The term he uses makes the slaves into the *benefactors* in this relationship! They are the patrons, the masters, the clients! In a word, Paul suggests the true nobility of
their service freely rendered to those who were their brothers
and sisters in the Lord but also their legal owners; the social
order is not changed but it is subtly subverted.

The problematic nature of wealth also figures in Paul's final
polemic against the false teachers (6:3–10, 20–21). Much of
this final outburst we examined in an earlier discussion (on
1:1–20). The opponents teach other doctrine (6:3) and are
generally "depraved in mind and bereft of the truth" (6:5).
Their knowledge is "falsely" so called (6:20). As we also saw
earlier, they are dangerous to the community above all
because of their "morbid craving for controversy and for
disputes about words" (6:4), since they specialize in "contra-
dictions" (or "antitheses," 6:20). Intellectual terrorism does
not build up the community in the truth of God's love. Rather,
it produces "envy, dissension, slander, base suspicions, and
wrongdoing" (6:4; see Rom 1:29–31). As Paul found from experience, the hostile attitudes revealed in constant verbal
battling results in the collapse of community: "if you bite and
devour one another take heed that you are not consumed by
one another" (Gal 5:15). Any teaching or dialectic which leads
to such results is self-condemned, for the "fruits of the Spirit"
and the "works of the flesh" are evident in behavior (see Gal
5:19–23; Eph 4:30–32), just as a good tree can be known from
its good fruit (Matt 7:17). Paul is particularly alert to the
damage such rancorous rhetoric can effect because of the delicate equipoise in which this community finds itself.

The new charge Paul brings against the opponents here is
that they are "imagining that godliness is a means of gain"
(6:5). In a word, they are trying to turn a profit from their
profession of religion. We remember that the ancient analysis
of vice divided it into three great modes: love of pleasure, love
of money, and love of glory. And although all vice ultimately
was one, a person could specialize in one or the other. It was

not uncommon, for example, for charlatans to avoid the grosser vices of pleasure-seeking but be avaricious. Others even avoided the love of money but still sought praise from others. Paul here accuses the opponents of wanting to become rich (6:9). The means was available; all they needed to do was charge the faithful for their teaching. Perhaps their success at this shows us why Paul was concerned that the community "pay double" its elders who taught and preached in addition to ruling. When rival teachers are making money by freelancing, it's tempting either to join them or imitate them.

In 6:9–10 Paul unrolls the list of evils exposed by the desire for wealth, for, he says, "the love of money is the root of all evils" (6:10). It is a craving which has led to the utter destruction of many (6:9). To appreciate the truth of this at more than the obvious level, we need to reflect a bit over what it means to be a lover of money in the sense Paul means. It is a compulsion which derives from the tragic identification of "being" (of human identity and worth) with "having." A person becomes more by having more. But this is an itch which grows greater the more it is scratched, for in fact no amount of "having" can ever make a person "be" more, not in the sense of what Paul calls real life (6:19), for that comes only as a gift from God, and it is the only true establisher of our identity and worth.

The sad thing about the love of money is that like all idolatries it ends by distorting both the object desired and the one desiring, for idols can only exist by devouring their worshipers. They have no life of their own and must live by the destruction of those who serve them. The distortion becomes acute when it infects religion itself. Then we not only meet the age-old perversion of wisdom found among the sophists of fitting the message to flatter those who pay the speaker but a corruption of an even deeper sort. For if religion itself is viewed as a "means of gain," it becomes itself a form of idolatry, in which its professors are "holding the form of religion but denying its power" (2 Tim 3:5). Why? Because while proclaiming the religious truth that we as creatures cannot increase our being by having, since all we are comes from God as gift, the preacher lives in a way which gives fundamental lie to that proclamation.

As before, Paul opposes to these misconceptions, "the sound words of our Lord Jesus Christ and the teaching which accords with godliness" (6:3). He does not in fact quote the sayings of Jesus here but could easily have done so: "Take heed, and beware of all covetousness; for a [person's] life does not consist in the abundance of his possessions" (Luke 12:15) or "You cannot serve both God and mammon" (Luke 16:13). He does, however, offer the "teaching which accords with godliness" both from Greek wisdom and from the deeper perception of faith. With many of his fellow Greek moralists, Paul agrees that the virtuous attitude toward material possessions can be summed up in the word "contentment" or "self-sufficiency" (*autarkeia*, 6:6). It denies the false equation between being and having. Only those possessions which are absolutely required for us to "be" at all are necessary, and with these, there is enough: "if we have food and clothing, with these we shall be content" (6:8). Paul expresses the same attitude in Phil 4:11–12: "Not that I complain of want; for I have learned, in whatever state I am, to be content [*autarkes*]. I know how to be abased, and I know how to abound; in any and all circumstances I have learned the secret of facing plenty and hunger." To be content, therefore, is to adopt a different measure for one's sense of identity and worth; neither can be changed by the vicissitudes of worldly existence. Paul deepens this perception further: "for we brought nothing into the world, and we cannot take anything out of the world" (6:7). Here, Paul echoes the sentiment of Job, who also added, "The LORD gave, and the LORD has taken away; blessed be the name of the LORD" (Job 1:21). The insight of faith is that all creatures stand before their Creator in the utter nakedness of contingency at every moment; nothing they do or say can fill up such emptiness before the awesome fullness of God. At the same time, faith asserts that there is no need to fill anything; the gift of existence which is fragile is also one of plenitude, for it comes from the God who "gives richly for our enjoyment" (6:17, author's translation).

For the last time, now, Paul tells Timothy to "avoid" and "shun" (6:11, 20) the perceptions and practices of the opponents. Instead, Timothy is to "pursue" a life of virtue (6:11), and we are not surprised to find in this list the characteristic element of "gentleness" (*praupathia*); he is to "fight the good fight of the faith," but gently (6:12). We recognize in these images a language now familiar to us from 2 Tim 2:3, 22; 4:7. As also in 2 Timothy, Paul proposes to Timothy the model of Jesus himself for imitation. The "good confession" which he makes before many witnesses is carried out in the presence of God and of "Christ Jesus who in his testimony before Pontius Pilate made the good confession" (6:13). And because Timothy makes his witness before the God "who gives life to all things" he can be confident that he will be able as well to "take hold of the eternal life" (6:12) which comes from him. But that life will become visible to humans only in "the appearing of our Lord Jesus Christ." So it is for Timothy now to struggle for the truth of the faith or, in an expression thoroughly characteristic of this letter, to "keep the commandment unstained and free from reproach" (6:14). This charge Paul places on Timothy in the sight of the one who will "be made manifest at the proper time," one praised in this stirring benediction (6:15–16):

> The blessed and only Sovereign
> the King of kings and Lord of lords,
> who alone has immortality
> and dwells in unapproachable light
> whom no man has ever seen or can see.
> To Him be honor and eternal dominion. Amen.

* * * * *

A consistent note runs through all of Paul's instructions in this chapter, challenging in a fundamental way much contemporary thought about human identity and worth. Pulling them together here may help sharpen the question this text poses to our own view of things and provide the stuff for building a sermon.

Whether Paul is talking about the rich or the slaves, the money-loving of the opponents, or the contentment of the virtuous person, he is basically saying one thing: human worth and dignity do not rely on the accidents of possession or social status. The person who is wealthy has no more "being" than one who is poor; the master has no advantage over the slave. And as we have seen elsewhere, the Jew has no advantage over the Gentile or the male over the female. The kingdom of God does not consist in food and drink. You can marry or not marry. If you are a slave you are free; if you are free you are a slave. Hunger or plenty, these make no difference for the person with *autarkeia*. Paul cuts the connection between the human condition and human worth. Because Paul has in effect said that it does not matter before the Lord if you are slave or free, it is usually understood that his is a conservative social ethic. To some extent this may be true. But it may also miss the point in two very important ways.

First, Paul's position does *not demand* an affirmation of the status quo. In fact it legitimates the change of social structure precisely because the social structure is not ultimate. Because it does not matter whether there are slaves or free, we can dispense with slavery altogether. Because both marriage and celibacy are gifts, we can choose either freely. Because the worth of a woman does not consist in her being head of the household, we are perfectly free to arrange things in our households so that she is at the head. The logic of Paul's radical severance of condition and calling can move either way. But our ability to effect change comes precisely from the understanding that *no social order* is equivalent to the kingdom of God or mandated by the gospel.

Second, much social thought in our world is far more inhibiting than Paul's, because it does tend to identify human dignity and the social condition. If women are really degraded if they do not teach, then—the logic runs—they *must* teach, they are not free to abstain. And if a person's essential worth is deprived in slavery, then—notice—only *when* free does that man or woman become a "real person." And the same for the dispossessed; if economic inequality is itself essentially degrading, then only within a perfect community of possessions is anyone just. When we identify our condition with our fundamental calling, we inadvertently limit our possibilities. Worse, we make our worth dependent on the realization of those conditions. If poverty makes a "man less a man" then it becomes impossible to choose poverty as a voluntary witness. Both the woman who is a real woman only in childbirth, and the woman who is a real person only because she carries a briefcase are in prisons. Only when we insist with Paul that none of these differences matters will we be free to change them as well as to affirm them.

TITUS

The Pedagogy of Grace
Introduction

The short Letter to Titus puts together the elements now familiar to us from 1 and 2 Timothy in still another distinctive fashion, sharpening our appreciation of the "pastorals" not as one message in three identical bottles, but as three individual letters, each with its own setting, literary shape, and significance. In this introduction, I will briefly survey the setting and literary structure. The significance of Titus will emerge from our closer examination of the text.

We know much less about Titus than about Timothy. He was a Greek and accompanied Paul on his trip to Jerusalem without being compelled to receive circumcision (Gal 2:1–3). If the variant reading in Acts 18:7 is correct, he may be the "Titus Justus" who was a godfearer in Corinth and whose house Paul moved to after being expelled from the synagogue—the connection, of course, is only speculative. It is certain that Titus worked extensively with Paul in his Aegean ministry, especially as his delegate in fundraising for the Jerusalem collection (see 2 Cor 2:13; 7:6; 8:16, 23; 12:18). According to 2 Tim 4:10, Titus also worked in Dalmatia. In this letter, he is stationed in Crete (Titus 1:5). The letter does not have the same personal warmth that Paul showed in 2 Timothy. Titus is a genuine child (1:4) but not a "beloved" one (see 2 Tim 1:2). Paul does pay special attention to the obligation of contributing money (in Titus 3:14), which reminds us of Titus' specialization.

We are not told elsewhere that Paul founded any churches on the island of Crete. In Acts 27:7–12 he passes by Crete as a prisoner on his way to Rome, but it appears that he barely had time to set foot on the island, much less establish a number of churches there. On the other hand, Acts is not exhaustive in its account either of Paul's personal movements nor of the establishment of churches under his direction. The establishment of churches in Galatia is a case in point, as is the existence of a church in Colossae. And if it were not for Paul's own statement in Rom 15:19 that he had preached as far as Illyricum, the mention of Titus working in Dalmatia would also probably be regarded as utterly fantastic. In any case, Paul's physical presence in Crete is not strictly required. The verb "I left" in 1:5 need not mean, "I left you physically"; it is more likely to mean, "I left you in that position. . . ."

As for Paul, at the time of writing he is apparently still active in the ministry. There is no suggestion of imprisonment, and he is making plans to winter in Nicopolis. If we knew which of the many towns by that name he meant, we would be better off. He also expects to see Titus there (3:12). Titus' appointment in Crete is, therefore, a temporary one. He is portrayed in characteristic fashion as a delegate/troubleshooter. The letter suggests that his talents along these lines will be stretched. Thus not only a youthful brand of Christianity (we notice that elders are still in the process of being appointed, 1:5), but its members come from a not encouraging segment of the population. Worse, these immature Gentile converts are being challenged by rival teachers, probably from Judaism (1:10) who are making considerable inroads among the faithful (1:11).

In its literary arrangement, Titus comes closer to the First rather than the Second Letter to Timothy. It has an extensive greeting (1:1–4)—one of the longest in the Pauline collection—but lacks a thanksgiving altogether; as in 1 Timothy, Paul gets immediately to business. The elements of paraenesis are minimal. The note of memory is sounded only in 3:1, where Titus is to "remind" believers of their duties. And as in 1 Timothy 4:12, the delegate is to present himself as a "model" to all the faithful (2:7). Paul does not appear as an example in any fashion. As for polemic, it is even sharper than in the other two letters; Titus is to take vigorous action against the opponents (see 1:11; 3:10). There is only the hint of the antithetical arrangement of the polemic which so dominated 2 Timothy: the opponents are contrasted to the overseer (1:7–10) and to Titus himself in 2:1 and 3:9–11. If the polemic in this letter has a literary function it is less to provide a contrast to the delegate as an ideal teacher than to highlight the necessity for the instructions which the delegate must communicate to the faithful.

We notice that the polemic forms a frame around the positive community instructions. These instructions—which deal, we should note, not with the internal life of the community so much as the believers' life in the world and household—form the bulk of the letter from 2:1 to 3:8. On either side, we find an attack on the opponents (1:10–16; 3:9–11). The polemic gives us a good sense for the threat being posed the churches from the outside. When we study the specific instructions carefully, we are struck by how their emphases correspond to this threat.

Perhaps the most surprising feature of Titus is the presence of two long theological warrants for the community instructions in 2:11–14 and 3:3–7. In these passages we find a high concentration of distinctively Pauline vocabulary and theological emphasis, with a special concentration on the educative power of grace itself. Even more than in 1 Timothy, the combination of the characteristically "Pauline" and the typically "Pastoral" forms a puzzle to those who are preoccupied with the issue of authorship and the place of these letters in the history of earliest Christianity. For those who read Titus for the instruction of the church today, its apparently artless collection of commandments turns out to be, on closer inspection, a coherent and challenging witness.

The Fight for the Truth (1:1–16)

For so short a letter and one so intent on business that it altogether omits a thanksgiving, Titus has a remarkably long and leisurely greeting, coming after Galatians and Romans in length, and like them elaborating aspects of the gospel and

of Paul's role as an apostle (1:1–4). In structure it most resembles the greeting in Romans: Paul identifies himself as a
servant as well as an apostle (1:1; Rom 1:1; see also Phil 1:1),
who has been entrusted with the proclamation of the gospel
(1:3; Rom 1:1, 5), a message which was promised in the past
but has come to full realization only in the present (1:2–3;
Rom 1:2–4). It is characteristic of Paul to craft his epistolary
greetings and thanksgivings so that they anticipate themes
developed later in the body of his letters. Thus, we notice the
importance of "the obedience of faith" and the "promise
through the scriptures" for the theological development in
Romans; the tension between "being saints" and "called to be
saints" for the exhortation in 1 Corinthians; the critical distinction between being called "not by man but by God" for
Paul's defense of his apostleship in Galatians; and (as we have
observed) the thematic role of "the promise of life" in 2 Timothy and the "command of God" in 1 Timothy.

In Titus as well, certain emphases of the letter are antici-
pated in the greeting. If in Romans it is the "obedience" of
faith which is stressed, here Paul emphasizes the *commonal-
ity* of faith. His mission is to "further the faith of God's elect,"
and Titus is his genuine child in a "common faith." This letter
will be much concerned with deviant teaching and the
troubles created by the "fractious person" (literally, the
"choosing person," *haeretikos*), who abandons the common
faith for a narrowed understanding of it. Paul therefore qualifies this faith as "according to the knowledge of the truth",
touching thereby on a theme important for these letters as
well as for others (see, for example, 1 Tim 2:4; 4:3; 2 Tim 2:25;
3:7; Rom 1:18, 25; Gal 2:5, 14; Col 1:5–6). This "knowledge"
(or "recognition") of the truth, furthermore, is not a simple
matter of intellectual assent but must "accord with godliness
(*eusebeia*)," that is, it must show itself in a certain character
of life. Much of this letter will consist in instructions about
how to put together faith in God with "godly lives" (2:12)
which manifest themselves in "good deeds" (2:14; 3:8, 14).

This "godliness," in turn, is governed by the "hope of eternal
life" given first by the promise and realized in the gospel.
Here is another characteristic emphasis of these letters. The
contrast between the true and false teacher is not simply a

matter of style; it is rooted in their respective hopes. The authentic Christian teacher is empowered by and hopes for true life (Titus 3:7), such as comes only from God the giver of life to all (see 1 Tim 1:16; 4:8; 6:12, 19; 2 Tim 1:1, 10). His life and ministry therefore stand in sharp contrast to those who profess God but put their hope in their own success or gain, and "deny him by their deeds" (Titus 1:16). Finally, the greeting emphasizes that the hope of life is manifested by "the word through the preaching" (1:3). Paul is very much preoccupied in this letter with the minister's skill in this "word" (1:9). No more than in Paul's other letters, therefore, is the greeting of Titus merely formal; it prepares us for the specific shaping of the message in response to the situation Titus faces.

Paul moves directly from the greeting to his statement of intention (1:5). He left Titus in Crete to appoint elders and "amend what was defective." The last phrase is somewhat obscure but can perhaps best be paraphrased in this way, "to build up properly what is now lacking." As we shall see, Paul's instructions in 2:1—3:8 have exactly that purpose. But if those specific instructions are to be more than transitory remarks in a letter, they must be personified and effectively taught by the local community leadership. Paul therefore turns first to this essential link of community identity and to the qualifications of those appointed as "elders in every town."

The list of qualifications in 1:6–9 is more than a little frustrating for those who are interested in the "church order" of the pastorals. This letter does not, indeed, have much "church order" at all; these four verses are the only ones devoted to the structure or life of the Christian community as such; all the other advice deals with the household and civic responsibilities of the believers. Nor are the qualities listed here much help in making clear any distinctions between the "offices" of elder and bishop. In fact, even though 1:6 begins with the qualifications for the "elder" (he must be blameless, the husband of one wife, with children as believers and under control), we discover in 1:7 that the list has shifted without warning to the qualifications of the "overseer." The need to be "blameless" is repeated, and so Paul may have had two offices in mind. On the other hand, vss. 6 and 7 are joined by the connective "for," which would make the "overseer" at best a special instance of an "elder." We cannot build an overly elaborate superstructure on so fragile a foundation. The community structure suggested by this passage corresponds rather well to the reconstruction I attempted when commenting on chapter five of 1 Timothy: a board of elders has a revolving office called the overseer, held in turn by one or more of the elders. Far more important to Paul than their respective job descriptions is the *character* of the elder/bishop, to which we now turn.

It is not surprising to find that the qualities listed here correspond in large measure to those found in 1 Tim 3:1–7. In both we find that the overseer is to be blameless and have only one wife; to be a man of self-control, not a drunkard or violent person or lover of money; a person of hospitality. In Titus 1:7 the overseer is called "God Steward" (*oikonomos tou theou*), which is lacking in 1 Timothy. The household steward is certainly not as exalted as the *oikodespotes* (lord of the household) to whom he is answerable. But the image of a "manager" of the household nicely expresses the sort of practical functions Paul envisages for these leaders (see also 1 Cor 4:1; 1 Peter 4:10; Luke 12:42).

The list of qualifications in Titus also differs from that in 1 Timothy in some important respects. These small differences give us some initial clues to the situation of the churches in Crete. 1 Timothy was addressed to an established church in Ephesus. Paul can therefore demand that the overseer not be a new convert (neophyte, 1 Tim 3:6). This would be an impossible demand in Crete, since this is a series of newly founded churches; everyone in them is a "new convert." The stipulation is therefore lacking in Titus. Likewise, the list in 1 Timothy stresses the demeanor and public role of the overseer; that he possesses internal dispositions appropriate to them can largely be taken for granted; thus, it is desirable that he be "temperate" and "dignified" (1 Tim 3:2). In Titus Paul has to spell out a bit more some basic virtuous attitudes: the overseer is to be "upright, holy, and self-controlled" (Titus 1:8).

Three differences in particular point us to the distinct situation presupposed by each letter. In 1 Tim 3:3 the overseer is to be "gentle, not quarrelsome," which is thoroughly consistent with Paul's overall ideal of the Christian teacher. But in Titus 1:7 we read that the overseer is not to be "arrogant or quick-tempered." The terms in Greek are exceptionally harsh, particularly the last, which could be translated as "wrathful." The distance between "not quarrelsome" and "wrathful" is considerable, and so is that between these social settings. We are in a situation where even for the bishop a highly polished finish of civility is not to be presumed. Likewise in 1 Timothy, the sign of good managerial prowess is the overseer's rule over his household, demonstrated by his children being submissive and respectful (1 Tim 3:4). But in Titus 1:6 Paul stipulates that the elder's children not only be believers (*pista*) but that they not be "open to the charge of being profligate or insubordinate." Clearly it cannot be taken for granted that the elder's own children will be converts to the faith. We are at a stage where Christianity is still much more "intentional community" than "church." Worse, the elder's children may be the sort who could be arrested for carousing or for criminal activity—so strong are the terms in Greek. Finally, in 1 Tim 3:3, Paul wants the overseer to be an "apt teacher"; no need to spell out what that entails. In Titus that qualification is spelled out as though to beginners: the bishop is first to be one who "holds fast to the sure word as taught." He is not an innovator but one who clings to the instructions he has received. Then, if he holds to this teaching, he can "exhort (the faithful) with healthy teaching" (author's translation), and he can "confute those who contradict it" (Titus 1:9). The bishop is, in other words, to continue the work of teaching and refutation which Titus is now performing.

The reason why such refutation is necessary is taken up next by Paul (1:10–16), which brings us again to the perennial problem of figuring out who the troublemakers are and how their propaganda affects the shaping of Paul's advice to Titus. As I have noted more than once, it is notoriously difficult to disentangle specific charges (and therefore perhaps historical evidence) from stereotyped polemic (and therefore largely rhetorical effect).

We can assume such slanders as that the opponents are "empty talkers and deceivers" (1:10) and that they engage in "stupid controversies" (3:9) are standard, as well as the charge that they "teach what they ought not" (1:11, author's translation) and preach but do not practice (1:16). We can be less certain about the charge that they teach for "base gain" (1:11); the frequency of this rebuke does not automatically preclude its occasional accuracy. We can, on the other hand, be sure of this: the opponents are active, proselytizing, and enjoying considerable success among these new converts in Crete. Paul says that they are "upsetting whole families" (1:11), and this fact is of first importance for grasping the rest of the letter.

Far less clear to us at this distance is the origin of the opponents, their relationship to the community, and their precise doctrine. Any reconstruction must be tentative, yet the risk must be taken if the particularly sharp response of Paul is to be appreciated. Three main pieces of evidence need to be weighed. First, Paul assumes that some members of the community are actively or passively involved in the deviance. He speaks of them as being "insubordinate" (the same word used of the elder's children in 1:6) and tells Titus to silence them (1:11) and "rebuke them sharply, that they may be sound in the faith" (1:13). The picture is of members of churches who are "giving heed to" (1:14) other teachers and doctrines yet can still be reached and brought back to a proper understanding or "sound teaching." Later on, Paul says "a man who is factious, after admonishing him once or twice, have nothing more to do with him" (3:10).

The second piece of evidence about the opposition is that it is being fomented by teachers, "especially those from the circumcision" (*hoi ek peritomes*, 1:10, author's translation). This expression is found only three other times in the entire NT, where it refers to Christians of Jewish origin and conviction (Acts 10:45; 11:2; Gal 2:12). One of their strongest convictions was that Gentile converts should be required to be circumcised and observe the law of Moses, including its regulations for purity (see Acts 15:1, 5). The authorities on the other side of this debate, therefore, seem to be messianist Jews. What was their teaching? It involves what Paul calls "Jewish myths" and "commandments," which have to do with distinguishing between what is clean and unclean (1:14). The opponents, furthermore, claim to "know God" (see Rom 2:18), and Paul says that they engage in "genealogies" and "quarrels over the law" (3:9). We have here a situation remarkably close to that which Paul faced in the Galatian churches: fresh Gentile converts are overwhelmed by the superior claims to wisdom and rigor purveyed by propagandists for Torah, and they become "judaizers," that is, Gentile Christians who wish to live "like Jews" (Gal 2:14), by being circumcised and observing dietary and ritual commandments.

The third and most puzzling piece of information is provided by Paul's citation of the epigram—attributed to Epimenides—concerning the native population of Crete, slandering them as "always liars, evil beasts, lazy gluttons" (1:12). Not only does Paul dignify this as a statement of a prophet but one made by "their own," that is, a fellow Cretan. But is he referring this to the Jewish-Christian teachers, native Cretans, or both?

The pieces are difficult to place back into the historical puzzle, but even as fragments they give us a rather clear general picture of the crisis Titus faced in Crete and the reasons for Paul's vigorous response.

First, this was a Christianity which was new and immature. Second, it was not only planted among Gentiles who lacked the moral instructions of Torah as part of their heritage but even—as all the evidence suggests—lacked the rudiments of civilized behavior. Third, their moral callowness was exploited by aggressive Jewish-Christians who offered these half-formed Gentile converts a highly sophisticated code of behavior. It was precisely the chaotic former life of these converts—of which we will shortly learn more—which made the detailed and rigorous demands of the law attractive, particularly if they could be supported by antiquity (genealogies) and divine etiology (myths). Fourth, the challenge for Paul and Titus was to provide guidelines for moral behavior without capitulating to a Christian legalism. In Galatians Paul invoked the normative power of the Spirit. Here he will build on the educative power of grace.

But first he brusquely rejects the pretensions of the Judaizers. Their commandments are those of people "who reject the truth" (1:14; see Paul's insistence on "recognition of the truth" in 1:1). Their minds and consciences are corrupted (1:15)—notice the same contrast between the demands of code and conscience that we saw in 1 Tim 1:3–11. Most important for the moralist, their discussions do not lead to anything *useful.* They are detestable and faithless, yes, but most of all they are "unfit for any good deed" (1:16). Paul will shortly show, in contrast, how grace instructs people in a life filled with "good deeds." Finally, as in 1 Tim 1:8–11, Paul offers a thumbnail clarification of the issue of clean and unclean, adopting again the "strong" position that it is moral intentionality (conscience) which fundamentally determines the moral character of human action, not a code of classification: "to the pure all things are pure." In contrast, if one operates with a foolish mind or a corrupt conscience, then "nothing is pure." This is not only "healthy teaching"; it is also strong medicine.

*   *   *   *   *

So compressed and elliptical is this opening section of Titus and so apparently defined by its historical circumstances that we might wonder whether it can speak to us at all. How can we preach this material? Yet just the specific dimensions of that long-ago crisis, as well as Paul's response to it, provide surprising light for a problem of increasing importance in our world and an apt topic for preaching: the confusion of faith and fanaticism.

Many of us who live more or less conventional lives in the church are astonished at the degree to which our age has become one of fanaticism. There seems to be little separating passionate, even violent behavior, and the most intense commitment to religious or ideological beliefs. In fact, the two seem increasingly to go together, so that the true believer is also the most committed to extremes of violence against "nonbelievers." The connection between faith and fanaticism is not found only among Shiite terrorists. In American culture, many Christian parents have had their children leave home and join new cults. To us this often seems an incomprehensible action. Such groups appear to offer nothing but a bizarre set of "myths" while demanding great personal rigor and dedication. We are puzzled when persons we know leave their homes for such highly structured, "confining" ways of life. We don't see how people raised in the climate of liberal, enlightened values could be so easily gulled.

What many of us have failed to realize, even within the church, is that our conventional liberal values have too often become not much more than an incoherent mass of warm feelings and right-minded sentiment, with little real coherence or conviction and still less passion. We have not perceived that children raised in an atmosphere we regard as enlightened and tolerant do not see it as liberating but as imprisoning in the most frightening way. They see us and themselves as lost in a miasma of moral uncertainty and confusion. Such young people also have often—quite unknown to their parents—already experienced the extremes of pleasure and passivity readily available in our culture. They have often already experienced the level of moral indolence attributed to the Cretans, as "liars, evil beasts, lazy gluttons." Yet within them the moral impulse has not died, it has only been stifled. They are hungry for moral clarity and spiritual purpose and sane social structure. If these are not available in their own world they will seek them in another. It is the atmosphere of moral chaos and lassitude which provides the best ground for conversion to a cult or the eager embrace of a moral legalism. No matter if the new doctrine is filled with myths and genealogies, the real appeal of cults and sects and morality movements is that they offer the possibility of a human life with structure, coherence, clarity, and above all, *choice* and *commitment.* The more intricate and repulsive the belief system the better for those who have had none, simply because any mythology offers the exhilarating and liberating experience of belief, of commitment to a truth and value beyond oneself.

I am suggesting, of course, that the fanatic edge to faith today and the great popularity of inhumane and intolerant creeds derive directly from a context of religious and moral instability. Many of our neighbors, many of us, are like those ancient Gentiles freshly converted from spiritual chaos; we are looking for a *way to live.*

Churches that see their young people abandon the fellowship either to drop out into the world of drugs and drink and crime or to fall into the world of sects and cults may be tempted to lure them back by making things easier, providing even more of what they think they want, whether field trips, parties, or special treatment. We might learn from Titus that what people most want is some value or cause which needs *them*, to which they can commit themselves. But how can we educate them in conviction and commitment? If we do not know ourselves what we believe and how we should act, what can we say to them?

An Education in Virtue (2:1–15)

How will Paul counter the inroads being made by the opponents? At first reading it does not seem much of a response at all. Rather than develop a full theological rebuttal or construct a competing legal code, Paul directs Titus to "teach what befits sound doctrine" (2:1). And reading further, we discover directions for behavior which are, to put it mildly, pedestrian. They are directed, furthermore, not at the community of Christians as such but at the basic familial unit of that culture, the household. The opponents are "upsetting whole families" (1:11) with their teaching about observance of the clean and unclean. Paul seeks therefore to strengthen the household by providing it with norms of behavior and also with an understanding of the source of those norms.

The chapter is framed by Paul's double exhortation to teach (2:1, 15). The second exhortation urges Titus to exercise his authority without allowing anyone to disregard him. The first provides an insight into the instructions themselves. When Paul tells Titus to teach "what befits sound doctrine" he does not thereby suggest that these household instructions are themselves that "sound doctrine." The gospel which announces what God has done for humans is "the word" which transforms them (1:3, 9). These instructions only spell out behavior *appropriate (prepei)* to those who have been educated by that word. As I have several times observed, this was a world in which concrete behavior was taken as self-evident proof of the "soundness" of moral teaching; the criterion is always "usefulness" (1:16).

For the first time in the Pastorals, we meet a genuine "table of household ethics" or *haustafel*, as scholars have come to

call this sort of instruction. In 1 Timothy all the commandments, with the exception of those given to slaves and the
wealthy, were aimed at the life of the community as such. 2
Timothy was devoted entirely to the attitudes and actions of
the delegate. But here Paul addresses the duties of persons
within the private household. It has become increasingly
clear that discussions of the mutual obligations of family
members and citizens of the city-state go back at least to Ar-
istotle's *Politics*. By the time of the NT they had become,
under the systematizing influence of Stoicism, fairly stan-
dardized. Since the structure of the society as a whole and of
the individual household was hierarchical, the main duties
of those on the higher ranks tended to be defined in terms of
responsibility and care, whereas those on the lower ranks
were exhorted in terms of submission and obedience. The
point of such discussions was to remind people of what was
"appropriate" behavior for each rank in the social order. The
"appropriate" was also most often "traditional." We do not,
therefore, expect to find innovation or daring in these instructions to older men (2:2) and women (2:3), younger women
(2:5) and men (2:6), and slaves (2:9–10).

Nevertheless, simply in formal terms, these instructions
have some distinctive features. Unlike the tables in Col 3:18–
4:1 and Eph 5:21–6:9, for example, we find no "pairings" of
husband/wife, parents/children, masters/slaves. In fact, the
opening instructions to older men and women scarcely appear to introduce household instructions at all; only when
the older women are told to instruct the younger do we begin
to recognize the *haustafel*. Since there are no pairs, neither is
there any reciprocity of obligation such as we find in Colos-
sians and Ephesians. Paul does not specify what members
owe each other but what they owe to their social roles. We
notice as well that by far the most attention is given to the
"lower orders" of women and slaves; the duties of husbands
and masters do not appear at all, and the only "parental" obligation is that of the older women. There are two possible
reasons for this focus. The first is that the community may
have been made up largely of these groups. More likely is the
possibility that these lower groups were most affected by the
teaching of the opponents and, therefore, needed more of a

reminder of their duties, since "whole families" were being upset (1:11). This would explain the peculiar emphasis in the advice to each group. Wives are told to be submissive to "their husbands" (2:5) and slaves to be obedient to "their masters" (2:9). They are not, in other words, to pay allegiance to authorities outside the family but maintain the structure and authority of the household.

Another distinctive aspect of the literary arrangement is the way Titus is told right in the *middle* of these instructions to be "in all respects a model of good deeds, and in your teaching show integrity, gravity, and sound speech" (2:7). We have learned already the significance of the delegate's example for the teaching of virtue, but the placement here is fascinating. The idea appears to be that by observing how Titus fulfills his role of ministry both in deed and speech, they all can learn to fulfill their respective social roles within the household. In the strictest sense of the term, Titus is here proposed as a "role-model." This explains as well the language used of him. He is to demonstrate in his actions, we see, "good deeds" (*kala erga*), which is just what Paul is trying to inculcate among all this people (1:16; 2:14; 3:8, 14). His teaching, furthermore, is to be (in the Greek) "a healthy word without reproach," which ties in to the emphasis throughout this letter on the way good behavior exemplifies and demonstrates the efficacy of the "word" they proclaim (1:3, 9).

One final observation on the formal arrangement of these instructions: three times, Paul interjects a statement of motivation. In 2:5 the behavior of wives is to ensure "that the word of God may not be blasphemed" (or "discredited," RSV). In 2:8 Titus' actions and speech should be so irreproachable that "an opponent may be put to shame, having nothing evil to say of us." In 2:10 the slaves are to "adorn the doctrine of God our Savior." This represents a high proportion of motivation to instruction. The most obvious reason for it is the concern for the community reputation and safety that we have seen so often displayed in these letters; if the community is seen as encouraging the breakup of the whole social fabric, it will eventually have to face the massive resentment and resistance of the social order's protectors. Another reason seems to be more important in this case. The way believers act in their various social roles demonstrates for all the world the efficacy and ethical value of "the word of God" (2:5), the "healthy word" (2:8, author's translation), the "teaching from God" (2:10, author's translation). This is particularly important because the Judaizers are insisting on a code derived from Torah for the regulation of life. Paul wants to show that the gift of God—expressed metonymically as "the word of God"—itself forms persons with such character that they behave properly; no purity code is required. Paul will argue just this in 2:11–14, and the repeated emphasis on the word of God in 2:5, 9, and 10 serves the rhetorical function of preparing for that theological warrant.

This high level of motivation, however, makes the actual contents of the instructions appear even more puzzling. They exhort people to the most ordinary, indeed, rudimentary sort of social behavior and moral attitudes. Why, we begin to wonder when we read through the catalogues carefully, should people need to be told these things? Either Paul was nodding badly when he wrote this, and Titus represents finally what critics of the Pastorals always protest, simply a reduction of the gospel to good manners, or there is something very important going on which requires more than a cursory examination. Only by patiently picking at the specific exhortations will we see which is the case.

No great shock in hearing the older men told to be "temperate, serious, and sensible," or that they are to live "sound in faith, in love, and in steadfastness" (2:2); these are appropriate enough virtues for the elderly, especially the capacity to "endure." The advice to the younger men also is short but to the point: they are to be self-controlled (2:6). In contrast to these jejune but pithy commands, the instructions to women and slaves are greatly elaborated and deserve closer reading.

Older women are to be reverent and avoid gossiping. Fair enough. But then Paul insists that they not be "slaves to drink" (2:3). The language here is quite strong, and whereas the qualification of the overseer not to be "given to wine" (1:7, author's translation) might be taken as formal, the repetition here suggests that drinking as an enslaving vice is a problem for this population. The older women also are to have a positive effect on their children, specifically on their daughters, the younger women. They are to be good teachers, or "teach what is good" (rsv) to them. As in all these letters, the pedagogical role of women is real but restricted to the private sphere and to the training of children. The content of their teaching is here summarized, and it is so elementary as to be at first bewildering. Who needs to be *trained* to "love their husbands and children" (2:4)? We notice that this is not a question of *agape* but of simple human affection (*philia*). Does not nature supply that? Why should this need to be taught? Then the younger women are to be sensible, chaste, and as we have seen, submissive to their own husbands. In the midst of this list occurs another "virtue" which the rsv translates as "domestic." This somewhat reduces its scandal to contemporary ears. Paul literally tells the older women to teach the younger ones to be good housekeepers (*oikourgoi*). Clearly, their realm of activity is to be the household itself.

The very ordinariness of these commands gives us pause. Why do younger women need to be taught these things? Why do the older women need to be reminded so to teach them? And why these particular things? We can work at these questions in reverse order. The instructions make it plain that the woman's role is in the household, but why is this so stressed? Some suggest that the reason is obvious: as in 2 Timothy where leisured women are entertaining and being seduced by charlatans, and as in 1 Timothy where young widows are going from house to house saying what they should not, we have here in Titus the rebelliousness of women against their social entrapment and in Paul's commands the reflex suppression of a patriarchal pastor. In a word, a first (or second) century fledgling women's liberation movement is squelched before it could prove disruptive of male supremacy. Such a reading of the evidence has something to recommend it but owes much more to our contemporary perspective than to the historical situation reflected in the letter. Perhaps the best evidence for this is provided by the instructions to the slaves, showing us that this is not specifically a male/female issue but rather one of the whole social order.

The instructions to slaves are equally elementary. They are to obey "their masters" (2:9). This submission is thoroughly generalized: they are to show "entirely good faith" (2:10, author's translation) to their masters "in every respect" (2:9). On the other hand, Paul provides two quite specific injunctions. They are not to be "refractory" (2:9) and they are not to "pilfer" (2:10). These are two very different levels and modes of rebelliousness. But we seem to have hit the nadir of Christian moral instruction when the adorning of the Word of God is specified in terms of not pilfering the master's silver!

Before entirely dismissing these instructions, however, we would do well to remind ourselves of the context to which they were issued. This is not the established church of Ephesus but a young and obviously unformed group of believers, uninstructed not only by Torah but also, it appears, by the civilizing influence of Greek culture with its own demanding ethos. We have observed repeatedly in this letter (and will do so again when commenting on chapter 3) that the native population from which the Christian movement drew its converts was rude and rebellious (1:12), proverbially so in the ancient world! This is a situation where the bishop's son might be arrested for profligacy or public disorder and where the bishop himself must be warned not to be "violent." The very obviousness and banality (to us) of the household instructions gives this section an air of verisimilitude and appropriateness. There are some situations, we must remember, where parents need to be instructed in the care of their children. Before one can talk about the finer feelings or modes of reciprocity between husband and wife, parents and children, one must try to see that the children are not being left exposed to die, that grandmother is not lying in a drunken stupor, that the adolescent son is not being arrested, and that the domestic servants are not ripping off the napkins. In a word, some level of social stability and civility is required, simply for the human enterprise to *be* human. And yes, there are situations in which the rudiments (the a-b-c's) cannot at all be assumed but must be taught.

The most remarkable thing about this passage is that Paul attaches to these quotidian commandments one of his most powerful statements of the good news (2:11–14). He does so in a deliberate and even provocative fashion, which gives us the essential insight into his thinking throughout this section.

The connection between the commandments and their warrant is explicit. First, we see that the behavior of slaves is to "adorn the doctrine of God our Savior," (2:10) and this statement is immediately picked up by "God the Savior of all people" (2:11, author's translation). More important, Paul joins the two sections with the connective "for," and this is the key. What God has done is the basis for what they are to be. The Christians of Crete are to demonstrate in their lives the usefulness of the teaching *because* of the nature of God's activity among them. How does Paul characterize that activity?

He says that the "grace of God" (or "gift") has appeared. The gift, therefore, is what grounds all the teaching. It is a gift from the God who wills *all people* to be saved, not just those who have Torah but also these pagans of rude and rebellious background. The critical link between the experience of grace and their behavior is established by the verb *paideuousa*. The RSV translates, "the grace of God trains us," which gets part of it. It misses, however, the rich resonances of the term *paideia* in Greek culture. *Paideia* meant an education in culture and in civilized behavior; it meant learning how to be a human being in the social world. In effect, Paul is saying that God's grace itself *educates* people in humanity.

To spell this out, he draws a contrast between the human condition before and after God's gift. They are now able to "reject" the life they lived before their conversion filled with "godlessness and worldly passions" and are able to "live sober, just, and godly lives in this world." This needs more careful examination than we can give it, but we can note at least this emphasis: Paul tells them that Christian life is not simply an experience nor yet simply the choice of a code of ethics. Between the gift and the action lies character, the reformation of the human person. And this is accomplished by the gift itself: what God has done is to empower in humans certain capacities for "sober, just, and godly" lives.

Paul has thus touched on the "already" aspect of Christian existence. The gift of God is already transforming them (for what is "education" if not transformation?), *in this age* (a better translation than "in this world"). But Christian existence is also characterized by a "not yet." They live this way, "awaiting our blessed hope, the appearing of the glory of our great

God and Savior Jesus Christ" (2:13). The important thing
about this last line is not what is usually debated, whether
Jesus is only called "savior" here or also "God." The important
point is that we have here no collapse of the eschatological
tension between the already and the not yet. Christians live
by a gift which is real and transforming but is not yet final.
Because they await a fuller revelation of God in Jesus, their
present social arrangements are not to be identified with the
"kingdom of God." In no fashion does Paul suggest (as the
writers of Qumran did) that the household of the believers
was somehow structurally a reflection or anticipation of a future order, a foretaste of "the kingdom of God." Their lives in
"this age" are as conditioned and contingent and transitory
as Paul stated them to be in 1 Cor 7:29–31. Their good behavior in the household is not therefore required because it has-
tens or reflects the kingdom but because such civil behavior
provides the minimum of stability and order for life to be "sober, just, and godly."

Having mentioned the coming of Jesus in 2:13, Paul now
further elaborates the structure of the gift of God and how it
should shape their own identity. The gift was given by God
through Jesus, but it was also a gift given by Jesus. In a thoroughly characteristic turn, Paul states simply, "he gave himself for us" (see Gal 1:4; 2:20), the shortest and most ancient
summary of soteriology (see Mark 10:45). The intention of
that saving act is then made explicit "that he might redeem
us . . . and purify us for himself as a people." Paul uses here
the traditional language of Torah. What God had done
through Moses for the Jews in the exodus, bringing the slaves
out of bondage and making them a people by the gift of Torah,
God had done for all people through the self-sacrifice of Jesus:
liberated them and given them an identity. It follows, therefore, that as the lives of Jews were shaped by the exodus experience and the norms of Torah, so should the lives of
Christians be shaped by the experience of Jesus' death and
resurrection and the Gospels' "sound teaching."

I left out of this summary the definition of what they were
saved "from" and what "for." They were liberated from "all
lawlessness." The RSV translates this as "all iniquity" but that
misses some of the precise point Paul is making. To be "with-

out law" or "outside the law" is to be in a "normless" condition, wherein behavior is regulated only by "tooth and claw and fang," which is just about what we have learned about this population. What the Christians have been liberated "for" corresponds to that previous condition: they are to be a people "zealous for good deeds." Finally and conclusively, we see that Paul specifies the work of the gift in them this way: God's intent is "to purify for himself a people" (2:14). Here is a situation in which Judaizers are claiming that only by code can one distinguish between clean and unclean (*katharos*, 1:15). In response, Paul says, "to the clean all things are clean" (*katharos*). Now we know that this is no abstract statement. The Christians of Crete do not need a code elaborating what is clean and unclean, for they have, by the gift of God, themselves been "made clean" (*katharizo*). They have been so changed that they are capable of living the most ordinary of lives in a transformed fashion. Their good deeds demonstrate the reality of the gift operative in their lives.

* * * * *

As so often in these letters, the careful and sympathetic analysis of the historical setting is itself the best help in seeing how the text might be heard in the churches today. My analysis has shown how a very specific sort of threat demanded an equally specific strategy of defense for the nurturing of a young and immature sort of Christianity. Certainly Christian communities today cannot adopt without more ado these specific household directives. Because Paul says that younger women should be good housewives obviously does not mean that women today should have only domestic functions. My earlier discussion on 1 Tim 2 suffices, I hope, on this rather obvious point. As social structures change (as they must to be functional for shifting historical circumstances) so do social roles and the ways of fulfilling them.

On the other hand, we should not simply assume that the North American nuclear family kinship system is the only one in the world. Perhaps in Ghana or Uganda ancestral kinship systems make Paul's advice pertinent and even progressive. I have no real knowledge of that. But I suspect that one of the hazards of precipitous censorship—refusing to read some passages because they do not match our situation—is its inevitable parochialism. The troubles of middle-class Americans are not necessarily those of the rest of the world's population; and the canonical texts must speak to all.

For that matter, this passage should make us be more self-critical about our own kinship system and how it works. In order to do this responsibly, we must remember that the family does not exist only for the convenience or for the emotional comfort it gives its members but has an absolutely critical role in civilizing the world—it is the primary locus of socialization and moral education.

If we ask, then, what sort of situation requires that women be told to love their husbands and children, we cannot assume that it is necessarily one far away and long ago. The evidence surrounds us in frightening fashion that our culture is one which hates children. It abuses them in ways barbarous people had not invented. Ours is a kingdom which increasingly has no place for children: not simply the retarded and the crippled and the ugly but all children. The culture of perpetual youth does not suggest that we like children; rather, it implies they are our rivals. We close our condominiums to them and our hearts to them. They are too weak, dependent, arbitrary and unpredictable, demanding. We have to give ourselves to them without much recognition or payment. So we rationalize turning over their care to others—"it is good for them," we say, perhaps meaning, "it is good for us."

These mild forms of rejection are only the visible symptoms of a hidden war we wage against children: not simply old-fashioned child exposure but abortion by the millions every year (not by poor welfare mothers who continue to bear children but mostly by the safe middle class for the sake of convenience). Then, child abduction, abandonment, neglect, child pornography, child sexual abuse, and battering—too much of this happens every day to be attributed only to moral monsters. We are the moral monsters, when we—men and women alike, for this is not the duty only of women but of men as well and in equal measure—abdicate our primary responsibility as human beings to civilization, which is to protect and nurture and educate the young in the best fashion possible, sacrificing our own interests so that human behav-

ior can continue in the world. If we do not give this role primarily to women (and, I repeat, we do not need to), then we
must ask who will do it? We cannot leave the essential mechanisms of civilization up to chance! It is time for us to reflect
on how much our blithe assumption (fostered by technologi-
cal comfort) that civilization can continue without our attending to it is valid; the barbarians are not only at the gate,
they live in our hearts. We need to think a bit more honestly
about *our* household arrangements. Is there really no connection between the broken homes and neglected homes and
homes in which roles and responsibilities and rules are con-
fused and subjects of constant conflict—is there no connection between this and our uncivil world? Can we hand over
our children to the care of others so blithely and still avoid
the collapse of the moral structures by which we would like
to live? Is Paul, after all, so wrong when he says that the gift
of God should educate us in humanity and that to be human
means *at the least* (not at the most) tending to the most fundamental requirements of the social order?

The Transforming Gift of God (3:1–15)

In this final chapter we come to see how Paul has all along
been developing a specific line of moral argumentation, perfectly fitted to the historical situation he addressed but trans-
latable to other ages as well. The chapter divides easily into
four segments: (1) a concluding statement on civic duties, (2)
a theological warrant, (3) a last warning against opponents
and how to treat them and, (4) personal notes. Since I have
treated the last two parts extensively in the reconstruction
of the letter's setting, I will pay exclusive attention here to
3:1–8.

As I pointed out earlier, the so-called table of household
ethics was actually part of a more extensive discussion of
moral duties which included consideration of one's responsibilities to the city-state; people were not only members of a
household but also citizens of the *polis*. Traces of this larger
topos can be spotted in Rom 13:1–7; 1 Tim 2:1–3; and 1 Peter
2:13–17 and are met here again in Titus 3:1–2. Because Paul
touches on the civic as well as the household duties of Christians, we understand that the concern for household ethics in

the previous chapter was not entirely defensive. Paul's overall interest is the context of civility within which the good news and, therefore, an authentically human life can flourish.

The instructions are brief but still cover two broad areas of civic responsibility: relations to rulers and relations with other people in the world. Toward civil authorities, we expect an attitude of "submission," and that is what Paul commands. In addition, he interiorizes and extends the meaning of that submission. It is not simply to be a passive bowing down before brute force but is to be matched by a spirit of obedience. They are also to be "ready for any good work." In the broadest sense, "good works" is what this letter is all about. In this case, I think Paul means the positive performance of civic obligations. Christians are not, in a word, simply to be "ruled" but are to be eager, active, even creative participants in the political order.

More than rulers make up the social world: Christians are also in contact with "all people." Paul says that their relationships with outsiders should not consist in evil speech ("reviling") or quarreling but should be filled with gentleness. They are to demonstrate meekness to all (3:2). This instruction is noteworthy on several counts. First is the characteristic Pauline insistence on gentleness as opposed to harshness. In 1 and 2 Timothy, he enjoined Christian teachers to show this quality; here the whole community is to be gentle and meek. It is not to imitate the quarrelsome manner of the opponents (3:2) for it is "unprofitable and futile" (3:9). Second, Paul here advocates a fundamentally open and positive view of outsiders. However strongly he urges the household to look to itself, he does not commend a sectarian attitude for the community as a whole or for its members. They are to live in the world and engage its social structures. They are not to treat others with what we would call "bad-mouthing" but with a reasonable and gentle demeanor. Third, Christians are to demonstrate these qualities to all people. The word translated as "show" by the RSV (*endeiknumi*) is often used for the providing of an example (see also 1 Cor. 12:31; Phil 2:17; 1 Tim 1:16; James 3:13). Just as God is one who wants "all people" to be saved, so is the community of faith to exemplify "for all people" the qualities of character consistent with that salvation. The community in this way models the "sound teaching" of the gospel.

As in 2:11 Paul now follows these rather mild directives with an extensive and grand theological affirmation so thoroughly Pauline in its sensibility that it provides an appropriate conclusion to this set of letters. Paul also, as in 2:11, joins the sections by the connective "for" (*gar*, 3:3), which establishes the theological statement as the warrant for the commands. We notice as well that the theme of gentleness in 3:2 is picked up by the "goodness and loving kindness of God our Savior" in 3:4. The theological statement is long and complex. It begins with a classic contrast between the "then" and "now" of the Christian experience: their previous human condition ("for we were," 3:3) is reversed by the action of God ("but when," 3:4). The nature of that divine intervention is then spelled out, together with the manner in which it has entered their lives (3:5–6), which leads to a description of their present status (3:7) and its behavioral corollary (3:8).

Paul portrays their former condition as one of unmitigated malignity. But he who was an observant Pharisee also associates himself with his readers in this misery (see also Eph 2:3); it is "we," not "you," who lived that way. Paul lists all manner of vice (3:3), and as we read through the catalogue we are impressed by the wretched compulsiveness of their former life. They were "enslaved" and "spent their days" in vice. No part of them was unaffected, not their minds (they were foolish, deceived) nor their emotions (they were driven by passions and pleasures) nor their will (they were disobedient, wicked, envious). Most of all, we perceive the pervasive misanthropy of their lives. They were "hated by [others] and hating one another" (3:3). This is, in fact, just the sort of vice list we would have expected to be applied to this populace from the hints we have had earlier in the text. Among them vice displayed its most savage forms. Without the constraints of the social order and individual commitment to it, competition for survival makes misanthropy functional.

God's intervention (3:4–5) has changed their situation in a radical way. Paul turns his attention to this "gift of God" (see 2:11; 3:7) that has "appeared." The shift in subject is most important: the state of misery was all their doing, the state of grace is all God's doing. Nowhere in Paul do we find a more emphatic statement of the gratuitousness of God's intervention for humans. Thus, he interjects at once: the change was not accomplished by "works of righteousness we had performed." The qualification has a double edge. It certainly reminds the Cretan converts that they have responded to a gift from another, not to their own natural progress in virtue—if in fact this group needed that reminder! It also rebuts the claims of the opponents that a pure life can be established by the observance of laws of purity—works of human "righteousness."

Because God has so freed them from their slavery to vice (3:3), Paul calls him "God our Savior" (3:4), and his work is simply stated: "he saved us" (3:5). We learn how to name God because of how he has shown himself to be in our lives. And how God shows himself to be corresponds with God's true nature—God "never lies" (Titus 1:2). This is why Paul emphasizes the manner of his saving action. It was through God's "mercy" that he saved us, not because we had earned it. Paul further describes it this way: "the goodness and loving kindness of God . . . appeared" (3:4). The word the RSV translates as "goodness" does not have so much an ethical quality as a psychological one: it is really the "sweetness" of God which is revealed. We are reminded of the cry in 1 Peter 2:3 (itself based on Ps 34:8), "you have tasted the kindness of the Lord." The term translated "loving kindness" is *philanthropia*, literally "love for humankind." Paul has scarcely used these terms arbitrarily: the way God has shown himself to us in gift is the way we are now able to live. If God has acted toward us in mercy, then we can be merciful, not envious; if he has shown us "sweetness" so can we be gentle and meek toward others, not abusive; if God has shown "love of humanity" and willed to save all people, then rather than "hate and be hated," we can show kindness to all people (3:2).

How, then, has this gift come to them? When Paul spoke of the gift of God in 2:11–14, he said that it came through Jesus "who gave himself for us" (2:14). Here Paul makes Jesus the source of their transformation as well. God "has poured out on them abundantly the Holy Spirit through Jesus Christ our Savior" (3:5b–6, author's translation). The language is extraordinarily dense because Paul draws together both baptism ("the bath of regeneration," 3:5, author's translation) and the gift of the Holy Spirit ("renewal in the Holy Spirit," 3:5) as the means (*dia* = through) by which they enter experientially into the gift of God's mercy. All this is also "through (*dia*) Jesus." As in the old doxology, it comes from God through Jesus in the Holy Spirit. Paul makes explicit use of the language of spiritual transformation: by baptism they are "reborn" and by the gift of the Spirit "made new." The gift, we learn, is real and changes people from one condition to another.

To describe their present status before God, Paul uses the characteristic language of Galatians, Romans, and Ephesians: "so that having been justified (made righteous) by his grace [gift], we might become heirs of eternal life, in hope" (see 1:2). Again we see the Christian "already" and "not yet." Saved from their lives of treacherous self and mutual destruction, they have not yet entered into the full realization of the kingdom. They live in hope, but their hope is secure (the "saying is sure") because it is based on the reality of the gift by which they already live, which is even now transforming them and "educating" them.

At the end, we encounter the paradoxical nature of Christian life in the world. Gifted by the very Spirit of God, the minds and hearts of believers are renewed, reborn with transformed minds and healthy consciences. The old self is taken off, a new one put on. With so transcendent and transforming a gift, we might expect that Christians would then lead extraordinary and spectacular lives, different in every way from other people. But such, Paul says, is not the case. Transformation by the Spirit does not make them superhuman, only authentically human, in right relationship with God and world ("righteous"). But when this happens, then all of reality is transfigured. The most ordinary and domestic of chores can become radiant with praise of God, can "adorn the doctrine of God our Savior" (2:10). Not bathos but the logic of grace itself allows Paul to move from this stirring recital of the kerygma (see 1:3) to the most mundane moral exhortation: "do good deeds, for they are useful to people" (3:8, au-

thor's translation). In some circumstances, just that capacity
is proof of transforming power.

* * * * *

We have found in Titus, beneath a sometimes unfamiliar
language, a profound articulation of the gospel which is un-
mistakably Pauline. Two aspects of Paul's perception call for
a fuller consideration and for homiletical development.

Life in the World. Titus poses in a sharp fashion the question of how Christians are to live in the world. Like the other
pastorals it maintains the distinctively Pauline eschatological tension: Christians live in an in-between time; the full realization of the kingdom is not yet theirs. Most significant in
this connection are the conclusions Paul does *not* draw from
that eschatological tension. He does not advocate a sectarian
attitude toward the world. He said in 1 Cor 5:9 that Christians were not to go "out of the world," and that is the point
of Titus as well. He certainly wants the community to shape
up its life in the household and its internal affairs, but it is
not to withdraw from personal contacts with others or the
structures of society. Paul may call the opponents corrupt and
speak of the converts' former life as one of hostility, but he
wants them now to be gentle and meek toward "all people."
They are not to speak ill of people outside the community.

Here is a question put to Christians who are comfortable
with an identity formed solely by opposition or who regard
all the world as lying in the grasp of Satan. Only by establishing a competing "Christian" order, they think, can they live
"holy lives." Enormous amounts of energy and devotion and
money are therefore poured into the construction of alternative social structures. From birth to death, and in every form
of commerce, Christians need never speak to or interact with
non-Christians. Ideally, there will be Christian education systems, Christian medicine, Christian science, Christian art-
work, Christian literature, Christian rock music, Christian
jewelry, placemats, and motels. This approach to Christian
identity is very close to that advocated of Paul's *opponents* in
this letter, who pushed a code of purity, so that by definition

some things and people and places would be "unclean" and
others "clean." It is hard to imagine an attitude more opposed
to Paul's own.

Paul wanted these young Gentile Christians to learn authentically human behavior from the gift of God itself. God's
love purified them and their conscience, so they could while
living in the world, see "all things clean" and do "good deeds."
They were to remain within the ordinary structures of the
world and fulfill their obligations to the household and the
empire. In this chapter, Paul encourages them to be participants in the political order, to do more than "show submission." They are also to "be ready for any good work." By
implication, he calls for Christians to work creatively within
the political process. They are not to drop out of the world in
sullen witness against its systemic corruption. Such abdica-
tion would allow corruption only to grow greater. Nor are
they to work single-mindedly for a state which is the perfect
realization of God's kingdom. Neither Paul nor they (then or
now) would have a real idea of what that would look like,
anyway. They are simply to work within the real, messy, complex structures of the political process as those who can "do
good deeds," because they are shaped by the gift of God.

The Experience of Transformation.   We pause over Paul's insistence on the transforming power of the Spirit. How strange
it sometimes seems to us, hearing such confident assertions
about the experience of God's grace. How remote it seems
from our own staid life in the Christian community. Yet Paul
unequivocally stresses the *reality* of this transformation. The
Spirit does transform our consciousness, does give us capacities we did not have before. Why are we so chary of celebrat-
ing this reality?

We do in fact know the transforming power of experience.
We do recognize that the experience of trust, acceptance,
love, and kindness can effect a deep change in one's person-
ality structure (character), so that a person formerly hostile
learns to accept himself or herself, as well as others, in trust
and love. We have all seen this. Why do we hesitate acknowl-
edging that this is the "gift of God" (grace) operative among
us? Because it is so ordinary? Yet for many the experience of

a single revelation of love is so powerful that it enables us also to speak of our lives in terms of a before and an after, of a change from fear and compulsion to freedom and joy. If when the human person Jesus "gave himself for us," God was at work to save, why is God not at work whenever any one of us "gives herself" for another? If such a gift between us can change our hearts, then we can be convinced even now, even today, of the experiential basis for our lives, of the work of God in our own story and the stories of others in the world.

My point here is a simple one. Paul says the "bath of regeneration" is a means by which the experience of grace reaches people. He surely meant more than the experience of a ritual bath. He meant by baptism the entry into a messianic people, a people living in gentleness and mutual acceptance and self-donation. The individual person initiated into the community should, can, experience the gift of God there. And if the community lives in this way, then it "demonstrates" to all people the power of the gift of God. The church is itself to make the goodness and loving kindness of God appear convincingly to all people.

Bibliography

The standard critical commentary with full bibliography is M. Dibelius and H. Conzelmann, *The Pastoral Epistles* (Hermeneia; Philadelphia: Fortress Press, 1972). More congenial to a reading from the standpoint of Pauline authorship, readable and reliable, is J. N. D. Kelly, *A Commentary on the Pastoral Epistles* (London: Charles and Adam Black, 1963). See also the following articles:

C. F. D. Moule, "The Problem of the Pastoral Epistles: A Reappraisal," *Bulletin of John Rylands Library* 47 (1965), pp. 430–52;

L. T. Johnson, "II Timothy and the Polemic against False Teachers: A Reexamination," *Journal of Religious Studies* 6/7 (1978–79), pp. 1–26;

R. J. Karris, "The Background and Significance of the Polemic of the Pastoral Epistles," *Journal of Biblical Literature* 92 (1973), pp. 549–64;

A. J. Malherbe, "Medical Imagery in the Pastorals," in *Texts and Testaments* (ed. W. E. March; San Antonio: Trinity University Press, 1980), pp. 19–35;

A. J. Malherbe, "'In Season and Out of Season': 2 Timothy 2:4," *Journal of Biblical Literature* 103 (1982), pp. 23–41;

R. H. Gundry, "The Form, Meaning, and Background of the Hymn quoted in I Tim. 3:16," in *Apostolic History and the Gospel* (ed. W. Gasque and R. P. Martin; Exeter: Paternoster Press, 1970), pp. 203–22;

M. J. Harris, "Titus 2:13 and the Deity of Christ," in *Pauline Studies* (ed. D. Hagner and M. Harris; Exeter: Paternoster Press, 1980), pp. 262–70; and

J. P. Meier, "*Presbyteros* in the Pastoral Epistles," *Catholic Biblical Quarterly* 35 (1973), pp. 323–45.